PRELIMINARY INVENTORY
OF THE
TEXTUAL RECORDS
OF THE

OFFICE OF THE

SURGEON GENERAL

(ARMY)

RECORD GROUP 112

COMPILED BY
Patricia Taylor

AND REVISED BY
Garry Ryan

HERITAGE BOOKS
2011

HERITAGE BOOKS

AN IMPRINT OF HERITAGE BOOKS, INC.

Books, CDs, and more—Worldwide

For our listing of thousands of titles see our website
at
www.HeritageBooks.com

A Facsimile Reprint
Published 2011 by
HERITAGE BOOKS, INC.
Publishing Division
100 Railroad Ave. #104
Westminster, Maryland 21157

Originally published
The National Archives
National Archives and Records Service
General Services Administration
Washington: 1964

International Standard Book Numbers
Paperbound: 978-0-7884-3477-8
Clothbound: 978-0-7884-8671-5

NM-20

GENERAL SERVICES ADMINISTRATION
NATIONAL ARCHIVES AND RECORDS SERVICE
THE NATIONAL ARCHIVES

Preliminary Inventory of the Textual Records
of the
Office of the Surgeon General (Army)

(Record Group 112)

Compiled by Patricia Taylor
and revised by
Garry Ryan

1964

INTRODUCTION

The Army Medical Service, as it exists today, dates from 1818, the year the office and the position of Surgeon General were established. During the Revolution there had been an analogous organization under a director-general, but it passed with the Continental Army. Except for the periods of the war scare of 1798 and the War of 1812, no really organized medical department existed from 1783 to 1818. A few surgeons and mates served at posts or with regiments under the orders of the post or regimental commander, but there was no common head or organization.

An act of April 14, 1818 (3 Stat. 426), regulating the staff of the Army, provided for a Surgeon General, an Assistant Surgeon General, and an increase in the number of post surgeons. One week later, on April 21, 1818, a War Department order directed that henceforth all reports, returns, and communications relating to medical matters should be made to the Surgeon General's Office and that all orders and instructions should be issued from his office.

From 1818 to 1963, the Surgeon General and the Surgeon General's Office have remained the administrative head and headquarters, respectively, of the Army Medical Service. The mission of this service, known as the Medical Department until 1950, is to maintain the health of the Army and conserve its fighting strength. To accomplish this mission the Army Medical Service develops plans and programs designed to provide the best possible medical service in war and peace. The present components of the service include the Medical Corps, the Dental Corps, the Veterinary Corps, the Medical Service Corps, the Army Nurse Corps, and the Army Medical Specialist Corps.

The records described in this inventory are in Record Group 112, Records of the Office of the Surgeon General (Army), and amount to about 4,240 cubic feet. They consist of five main aggregations: (1) records of the Surgeon General's Office proper; (2) records of the various subdivisions of that Office; (3) records of Army medical examining boards; (4) records of Army medical installations; and (5) records of various military units.

Other records in the National Archives relating to the Surgeon General's Office are in Record Group 94, Records of The Adjutant General's Office; Record Group 98, Records of U.S. Army Commands; Record Group 120, Records of the American Expeditionary Forces, 1917-21; and Record Group 160, Records of Headquarters Army Service Forces.

SURGEONS GENERAL

Joseph Lovell	Apr. 18, 1818-Oct. 17, 1836
Col. Thomas Lawson	Nov. 30, 1836-May 15, 1861
Col. Clement A. Finley	May 15, 1861-Apr. 14, 1862
Brig. Gen. William A. Hammond	Apr. 25, 1862-Aug. 18, 1864
Brig. Gen. Joseph K. Barnes	Aug. 22, 1864-June 30, 1882
Brig. Gen. Charles H. Crane	July 3, 1882-Oct. 10, 1883
Brig. Gen. Robert Murray	Nov. 23, 1883-Aug. 6, 1886
Brig. Gen. John Moore	Nov. 18, 1886-Aug. 16, 1890
Brig. Gen. Jedediah H. Baxter	Aug. 16, 1890-Dec. 4, 1890
Brig. Gen. Charles Sutherland	Dec. 23, 1890-May 29, 1893
Brig. Gen. George M. Sternberg	May 30, 1893-June 2, 1902
Brig. Gen. William H. Forwood	June 8, 1902-Sept. 7, 1902
Brig. Gen. Robert M. O'Reilly	Sept. 7, 1902-Jan. 14, 1909
Brig. Gen. George H. Torney	Jan. 14, 1909-Dec. 27, 1913
Maj. Gen. William C. Gorgas	Jan. 16, 1914-Oct. 3, 1918
Maj. Gen. Merritte W. Ireland	Oct. 4, 1918-May 31, 1931
Maj. Gen. Robert U. Patterson	June 1, 1931-May 31, 1935
Maj. Gen. Charles R. Reynolds	June 1, 1935-May 31, 1939
Maj. Gen. James C. Magee	June 1, 1939-May 31, 1943
Maj. Gen. Norman T. Kirk	June 1, 1943-May 31, 1947
Maj. Gen. Raymond W. Bliss	June 1, 1947-May 31, 1951
Maj. Gen. George E. Armstrong	June 1, 1951-May 31, 1955
Maj. Gen. Silas B. Hays	May 31, 1955-May 31, 1959
Lt. Gen. Leonard D. Heaton	May 31, 1959-

TEXTUAL RECORDS OF THE OFFICE OF THE SURGEON GENERAL (ARMY)

I. Central Office

A. Correspondence, 1818-1946

1. 1818-90 Period

NAME AND SUBJECT INDEXES TO PART (1871-89) OF SERIES 2. 20 vols.
   3 ft.
   Yearly indexes.

1

LETTERS AND ENDORSEMENTS SENT. Apr. 1818-Oct. 1889. 90 vols.
   21 ft.
   Arranged chronologically. The volumes for the period 1818-73
have name and subject indexes. For name and subject indexes for
the period 1871-89 see series 1.

2

NAME AND SUBJECT INDEXES TO SERIES 4. 6 vols. 4 in.
   Divided into periods.

3

LETTERS AND ENDORSEMENTS SENT TO THE SECRETARY OF WAR. Mar. 1837-
   May 1866. 6 vols. 1 ft.
   Arranged chronologically. For name and subject indexes see
series 3.

4

NAME AND SUBJECT INDEXES TO SERIES 6. 36 vols. 3 ft.
   Yearly indexes

5

LETTERS AND ENDORSEMENTS SENT TO THE WAR DEPARTMENT. Sept. 1862-
   Oct. 1889. 25 vols. 5 ft.
   Arranged chronologically. For name and subject indexes see
series 5.

6

LETTERS AND ENDORSEMENTS SENT TO MEDICAL OFFICERS ("MILITARY LETTERS").
   Sept. 1862-Sept. 1872. 18 vols. 4 ft.
   Arranged chronologically. Name and subject index in each volume.

7

LETTERS SENT BY THE ASSISTANT SURGEON GENERAL RELATING TO PERSONNEL.
   1869-83. 1 vol. 3 in.
   Arranged chronologically. Name and subject index.

8

NAME AND SUBJECT INDEXES TO PART (1862-89) OF SERIES 12. 39 vols.
   6 ft.
   Yearly indexes.

9

REGISTERS OF LETTERS RECEIVED. 1822-89. 62 vols. 15 ft.   <u>10</u>
    Arranged by period, thereunder alphabetically by initial letter
of correspondent's surname, and thereunder generally by date of
receipt. The entries are numbered consecutively.

REGISTER OF LETTERS RECEIVED REQUESTING DISCHARGES AND TRANSFERS OF
    MEDICAL DEPARTMENT PERSONNEL IN SERIES 12. 1864-65. 1 vol.
    1 in.   <u>11</u>
    Arranged chronologically within three subseries: By State of
the unit with which the person served; by State from which the person
came; and by the name of the Congressman making the request.

LETTERS RECEIVED. 1818-89. 530 ft.   <u>12</u>
    Arranged alphabetically by initial letter of correspondent's
surname and thereunder chronologically to 1870. From 1871 to 1889
arranged by year and thereunder arranged and numbered in chronological corder. For registers to these letters see series 10. For name
and subject indexes see series 9.

CORRESPONDENCE RELATING TO ARMY MEDICAL EXAMINING BOARDS. 1831-98.
    30 ft.   <u>13</u>
    Arranged chronologically. Most of this correspondence was
originally in series 12, 22, and 26.

LETTERS REFERRED TO THE SURGEON GENERAL BY THE WAR DEPARTMENT.
    Oct. 1860-Mar. 1861. 1 vol. 3 in.   <u>14</u>
    Arranged chronologically. Name index.

CORRESPONDENCE RELATING TO THE PROMOTION, DISCHARGE, AND RATING OF
    PERSONNEL ("CONFIDENTIAL FILE"). 1871-94. 1 ft.   <u>15</u>
    Unarranged. This correspondence was withdrawn from series 12
and 22.

CORRESPONDENCE REGARDING THE ORGANIZATION OF THE HOSPITAL CORPS.
    Feb. 1880-Mar. 1888. 2 vols. 1 in.   <u>16</u>
    Arranged chronologically.

CORRESPONDENCE WITH MEDICAL OFFICERS REGARDING FIELD MANEUVERS.
    1888-90. 1 ft.   <u>17</u>
    Unarranged. This correspondence was withdrawn from series 12
and 22.

        2.   <u>1890-1917 Period</u>

NAME AND SUBJECT INDEXES TO PARTS (1889-90) OF SERIES 12 AND 22.
    3 ft.   <u>18</u>
    Card indexes, arranged by year.

CORRESPONDENCE WITH MILITARY INSTALLATIONS, COMMANDS, AND UNITS
AND WITH CIVILIAN ORGANIZATIONS ("GEOGRAPHIC FILE"). 1917-46.   31
1,765 ft.
Arranged in four chronological subseries: 1917-27, 1928-37,
1938-44, and 1945-46. Each of the first two subseries is arranged
according to a subject-alphabetic classification scheme reproduced
as appendix I; each of the last two is arranged according to a
similar shceme reproduced as appendix II. Further arrangement for
each subseries is alphabetical or numerical and thereunder according
to the War Department decimal classification scheme.

SECURITY-CLASSIFIED CORRESPONDENCE WITH MILITARY INSTALLATIONS,
COMMANDS, AND UNITS AND WITH CIVILIAN ORGANIZATIONS ("GEOGRAPHIC
FILE"). 1938-46. 40 ft.   32
Arranged in two chronological subseries (1938-44 and 1945-46),
thereunder according to a subject-alphabetic classification scheme
(reproduced as appendix II), thereunder alphabetically or numerically,
and thereunder according to the War Department decimal classification
scheme.

CORRESPONDENCE RELATING TO PERSONS AND FIRMS. 1917-37. 12 ft.   33
Arranged alphabetically by name and thereunder chronologically.

B.   Telegrams, 1868-89

TELEGRAMS SENT AND RECEIVED. 1868-89. 3 vols. 4 in.   34
Arranged chronologically. Each volume has a name index.

C.   Endorsements, 1864-87

ENDORSEMENTS RELATING TO SUPPLIES AND ACCOUNTS. 1864-87. 1 vol.
3 in.   35
Arranged chronologically. Name index.

ENDORSEMENTS RELATING TO THE ASSIGNMENT, TRANSFER, AND DISCHARGE
OF MILITARY PERSONNEL SERVING IN THE MEDICAL DEPARTMENT.
Mar. 1865-Mar. 1866. 1 vol. 2 in.   36
Arranged chronologically.

ENDORSEMENTS RELATING TO REPAIRS OF POST HOSPITALS. 1872-74.
2 vols. 3 in.   37
Arranged by military department and thereunder by post.
Indexes to departments and posts in the volumes.

D. Reports, 1818-1919

   1. Inspection and Sanitary Reports

INSPECTION REPORTS OF MEDICAL FACILITIES AT ARMY POSTS. 1890-94.
   2 ft.   38
   Arranged alphabetically by name of post.

INSPECTION REPORTS SUBMITTED BY THE MEDICAL DIRECTORS OF THE
   MILITARY DEPARTMENTS RELATING TO MEDICAL FACILITIES AT ARMY
   POSTS. 1890-93. 6 in.   39
   Arranged alphabetically by name of department.

EXTRACTS OF INSPECTION REPORTS MADE BY THE INSPECTOR GENERAL'S
   DEPARTMENT RELATING TO MEDICAL FACILITIES AT ARMY POSTS. 1891-94.
   3 in.   40
   Arranged by enclosure number. Formerly file number 2976 of
series 22.

SANITARY INSPECTION REPORTS. 1892-94. 6 in.   41
   Arranged alphabetically by name of post.

SPECIAL SANITARY REPORTS. June 30, 1893. 6 in.   42
   Arranged alphabetically by post (S-V only).

INSPECTION REPORTS OF SANITARY CONDITIONS DURING THE SPANISH-
   AMERICAN WAR. 1898-99. 6 in.   43
   Arranged numerically.

MONTHLY SANITARY REPORTS OF MILITARY POSTS. 1914-16. 10 in. 44
   Arranged alphabetically by name of post and thereunder by month.

   2. Miscellaneous Reports

NAME INDEX TO CONTRACT SURGEONS MENTIONED IN PART (1839-74) OF
   SERIES 46. 2 vols. 2 in.   45

REPORTS TO THE SECRETARY OF WAR RELATING TO OFFICE ACTIVITIES,
   PERSONNEL, AND EXPENDITURES. 1818-94. 2 vols. 2 ft.   46
   Arranged chronologically. Name and subject index in each
volume.

WEEKLY REPORTS OF LETTERS ADDRESSED OR REFERRED TO THE SURGEON
   GENERAL. May 1833-July 1840. 2 vols. 2 in.   47
   Arranged chronologically.

REPORTS OF VARIOUS POST HOSPITALS. 1862-65; 1868. 1 in.   48
   Arranged by name of hospital.

PERSONNEL ORDERS OF THE SURGEON GENERAL'S OFFICE. 1944-45. 1 in.   60
   Arranged chronologically.

SUBJECT INDEXES TO WAR DEPARTMENT GENERAL ORDERS AND CIRCULARS
   ISSUED 1883-91. 3 vols. 1/2 in.   61
   Divided into periods.

SUBJECT INDEXES TO PART (1861-80) OF SERIES 63. 2 vols. 3 in.   62
   Divided into periods.

CIRCULARS AND CIRCULAR LETTERS OF THE SURGEON GENERAL'S OFFICE.
   1861-85. 7 vols. 1 ft.   63
   Arranged chronologically.

MANUSCRIPT AND PROOF OF SURGEON GENERAL'S OFFICE CIRCULAR NO. 6 OF
   1865. 1 in.   64

CIRCULARS AND DECISIONS OF THE SURGEON GENERAL. Nov. 1887-Apr. 1892.
   1 vol. 1 in.   65
   Arranged chronologically.

CIRCULARS OF THE SURGEON GENERAL'S OFFICE. July 1889-Jan. 1905.
   2 vols. 2 in.   66
   Arranged chronologically in each volume. One volume contains
circulars dated January 1895-March 1900, some of which are dupli-
cated in the other volume.

CIRCULAR LETTERS OF THE SURGEON GENERAL'S OFFICE. 1919-44. 2 ft.   67
   Arranged chronologically.

OFFICE MEMORANDA OF THE SURGEON GENERAL'S OFFICE. 1917-45. 1 vol.   68
   and loose papers. 2 ft.
   Volume (1918) is unarranged; loose papers arranged chronologically.

"MISCELLANEOUS LETTERS AND MEMORANDA" OF THE SURGEON GENERAL'S
   OFFICE. 1917-20. 2 ft.   69
   Arranged chronologically.

WAR DEPARTMENT TECHNICAL BULLETINS (MED 1-200). 1943-45. 9 in.   70
   Arranged numerically.

ARMY MEDICAL BULLETIN (PERIODICAL). 1922-49. 4 ft.   71
   Arranged chronologically. Name changed to The Bulletin of the
U.S. Army Medical Department in November 1943.

DENTAL BULLETIN (PERIODICAL). 1933-43. 1 ft.   72
   Arranged chronologically.

SAMPLE BOOK OF BLANK FORMS IN USE IN THE MEDICAL DEPARTMENT DURING
  THE 1890'S. 1 vol. 1/2 in.

MEDICAL DEPARTMENT "OBSOLETE" FORMS 1-376. 1917-44. 3 ft.
  Arranged numerically. Included are a few War Department forms
relating to the Medical Department.

  F. Records Relating to Military Personnel,
        1775-1947

    1. Regular Army Personnel

      a. Surgeons and Assistant Surgeons

NAME INDEX TO VOLUME 2 OF SERIES 76. 1 vol. 1/4 in.
  Arranged alphabetically by initial letter of applicant's
surname.

LIST OF APPLICANTS FOR APPOINTMENT TO THE MEDICAL DEPARTMENT.
  1816-54. 3 vols. 3 in.
  Arranged chronologically by date of application. Volume 1 has
a name index. For a name index to volume 2 see series 75. Volumes
2 and 3 contain lists of applicants by State. Volume 3 includes the
merit rolls for 1832-60 (see series 77) and a list of contracts of
the Medical Department, 1838-46. The latter is arranged chronologically by date of contract.

REPORTS OF EXAMINATIONS OF CANDIDATES FOR APPOINTMENT AS REGULAR ARMY
  SURGEONS ("MERIT ROLLS"). 1860-88. 1 in.
  Arranged chronologically by the date the Army medical board
convened. There is a name index of candidates. Merit rolls for
1832-60 are in volume 3 of series 76.

REGISTER OF APPLICANTS FOR POSITIONS WITH THE MEDICAL DEPARTMENT.
  1865-68. 1 vol. 1 in.
  Arranged by position applied for and thereunder chronologically.

CASE FILES OF CANDIDATES FOR APPOINTMENT TO THE MEDICAL CORPS WHO
  WERE EXAMINED BY ARMY MEDICAL EXAMINING BOARDS. 1890-1917.
  290 ft.
  Arranged alphabetically by name of candidate.

PERSONAL HISTORIES OF CANDIDATES SEEKING APPOINTMENT TO THE
  MEDICAL CORPS. 1894-1917. 6 ft.
  Arranged alphabetically by name of candidate.

REGISTER OF APPLICANTS SEEKING APPOINTMENT AS ASSISTANT SURGEONS.
   1898-1901. 1 vol. 1/2 in.   81
   Arranged chronologically by date of invitation to appear for
examination.

PROFESSIONAL QUALIFICATION CARDS OF CANDIDATES SEEKING APPOINTMENT
   AS ARMY MEDICAL SURGEONS. 1916-18. 1 ft.   82
   Arranged alphabetically by name.

LIST OF OFFICERS IN THE MEDICAL DEPARTMENT. 1775-1892. 1 vol.
   2 in.   83
   Arranged alphabetically by name of officer.

MILITARY SERVICE CARDS OF REVOLUTIONARY WAR MEDICAL OFFICERS.
   1775-1819. 6 in.   84
   Arranged alphabetically by name of officer.

NAME INDEX TO PART (1870-90) OF SERIES 86. 1 vol. 2 in.   85
   Arranged alphabetically by initial letter of medical officer's
surname.

REGISTERS OF MILITARY SERVICE OF MEDICAL OFFICERS. 1806-20; 1849-
   1902. 11 vols. 2 ft.   86
   Each volume arranged alphabetically by initial letter of officer's
surname. Each volume has a name index. For a separate index see
series 85.

MILITARY SERVICE CARDS OF MEDICAL OFFICERS. 1812-62. 4 in.   87
   Arranged alphabetically by name of officer.

MILITARY SERVICE CARDS OF RETIRED OR DECEASED MEDICAL OFFICERS.
   1813-1914. 1 ft.   88
   Arranged alphabetically by name of officer (A-R).

MILITARY SERVICE CARDS OF MEDICAL OFFICERS. 1860-1917. 3 ft.   89
   Arranged alphabetically by name of officer.

REGISTER OF MILITARY SERVICE OF MEDICAL OFFICERS AND CONTRACT
   SURGEONS. 1876-79. 1 vol. 2 in.   90
   Arranged alphabetically by initial letter of name. For registers
of military service of contract surgeons for 1898-1914 see series
138.

MILITARY SERVICE CARDS OF REGULAR ARMY OFFICERS OF THE MEDICAL CORPS.
   1894-1917. 10 ft.   91
   Arranged alphabetically by name in two subseries: medical
officers on active duty and medical officers separated from the
service.

SUMMARY DATA CARDS RELATING TO THE POSTS AND STATIONS OF MEDICAL
OFFICERS. 1825-1909. 2 ft.   92
Arranged alphabetically by name of post or station (A-R), and
thereunder by date of officer's arrival at post.

LISTS SHOWING THE SERVICE AND STATIONS OF MEDICAL OFFICERS. 1829-33.
1 vol. 1 in.   93
Also contains lists of vaccine shipments and the service and
stations of Quartermaster officers.

STATION BOOKS OF MEDICAL OFFICERS. 1857-1902. 2 vols. 3 in.   94
One volume shows officers at permanent posts, and the other
those at temporary camps and stations. Each is arranged alphabetically by name of post or camp, and thereunder chronologically
by date of officer's arrival at post.

MONTHLY STRENGTH RETURNS OF THE MEDICAL DEPARTMENT. 1831-57;
1863-1905; 1908-12. 15 vols. 1 ft.   95
Arranged chronologically.

MONTHLY STRENGTH RETURNS OF MEDICAL OFFICERS IN VARIOUS COMMANDS.
1888-90; 1893-97; 1900-16. 9 ft.   96
Arranged chronologically by month and thereunder by command.

LISTS SHOWING THE SERVICE, LEAVE, EXAMINATIONS, AND STATIONS OF
MEDICAL DEPARTMENT OFFICERS. 1854-57. 1 vol. 1/2 in.   97
Entries grouped by subject and arranged thereunder chronologically. The volume also includes lists of shipments of medical
supplies and periodicals to Army posts.

REPORTS CONCERNING THE EFFICIENCY AND EXPERIENCE OF MEDICAL OFFICERS.
1913; 1915. 7 in.   98
Arranged by year and thereunder alphabetically by name of officer.

REGISTERS OF MEDICAL OFFICERS OF THE REGULAR ARMY ARRIVING AT THE
SURGEON GENERAL'S OFFICE. 1848-89. 2 vols. 3 in.   99
Entries arranged chronologically by date of officer's arrival.

REGISTER OF DEATHS OF REGULAR ARMY MEDICAL OFFICERS. 1861-96.
1 vol. 1 in.   100
Arranged alphabetically by initial letter of officer's surname.
For supplementary information see series 128.

b. Dental Surgeons

CASE FILES OF PERSONS EXAMINED FOR APPOINTMENT AS DENTAL SURGEONS.
1900-17. 35 ft.   101
Arranged alphabetically by name of candidate.

MILITARY SERVICE CARDS OF DENTAL SURGEONS. 1911-17. 4 in.   102
   Arranged alphabetically by name of officer.

c. Nurses

       For records of Spanish-American War contract nurses
(1898-1901) see series 147-150. The records of the Army School of
Nursing comprise series 287.

HISTORICAL FILES OF THE ARMY NURSE CORPS. 1900-47. 6 ft.   103
   Unarranged.

CASE FILES OF CANDIDATES SEEKING APPOINTMENT AS ARMY NURSES. 1898-
   1917. 34 ft.   104
   Arranged alphabetically by name of nurse in two subseries:
successful candidates and unsuccessful candidates. Includes some
subsequent correspondence of Army nurses.

REGISTER OF MILITARY SERVICE OF MEMBERS OF THE ARMY NURSE CORPS.
   1901-2. 1 vol. 3 in.   105
   Arranged alphabetically by initial letter of surname. The
volume includes a name index.

MONTHLY STRENGTH RETURNS OF NURSES. 1899-1917. 7 ft.   106
   Arranged chronologically and thereunder by station.

STATION BOOKS OF NURSES. 1899-1903; 1911-16. 2 vols. 4 in.   107
   Entries in each volume arranged by station and thereunder
chronologically by date of nurse's arrival at post.

ANNUAL EFFICIENCY REPORTS ON NURSES. 1898-1917. 9 ft.   108
   Arranged chronologically by year and thereunder by station.

LIST OF NURSES WHO SERVED WITH THE ARMY NURSE CORPS DURING WORLD
   WAR I (1917-21). 1 vol. 1 in.   109
   Arranged alphabetically by name of nurse.

d. Veterinaries

CASE FILES OF CANDIDATES SEEKING APPOINTMENT TO THE VETERINARY
   CORPS. 1916. 5 ft.   110
   Arranged alphabetically in part.

e. Hospital Stewards and Hospital Corpsmen

"REGISTER OF EXAMINATIONS" FOR THE POSITIONS OF HOSPITAL STEWARD AND
    ACTING HOSPITAL STEWARD. 1887-91. 1 vol. 1 in.   111
    This volume has three sections: an alphabetical list of candi-
dates, correspondence relating to the examinations, and copies of
examination questions.

NAME INDEX TO SERIES 113. 1 vol. 1/2 in.   112
    Arranged alphabetically.

REGISTERS OF MILITARY SERVICE OF HOSPITAL STEWARDS. 1856-87. 8 vols.
    1 ft.   113
    Each volume arranged chronologically and thereunder by name of
hospital steward. Name index in each volume.

LIST OF HOSPITAL STEWARDS AND ACTING HOSPITAL STEWARDS SHOWING DATES
    OF APPOINTMENT AND DISCHARGE. 1862-1913. 2 vols. 1 in.   114
    Arranged chronologically by date of appointment.

LIST OF ENLISTED MEN WHO SERVED AS SECOND- AND THIRD-CLASS HOSPITAL
    STEWARDS. 1870-87. 1 vol. 1/2 in.   115
    Arranged alphabetically by name of soldier.

LIST OF HOSPITAL STEWARDS ON DUTY AT VARIOUS POSTS. 1870-87. 1 vol.
    1 in.   116
    Arranged alphabetically by name of post and thereunder chronologi-
cally by dates of service at post.

DESCRIPTIVE BOOK OF HOSPITAL STEWARDS. 1863-67. 1 vol. 1 in.   117
    Arranged alphabetically by initial letter of surname. Name
index.

RETURNS OF PERSONNEL AND EQUIPMENT OF THE HOSPITAL CORPS. 1887-96.
    78 vols. 10 ft.   118
    Arranged chronologically by year and thereunder alphabetically
by name of post.

MONTHLY POST RETURNS OF PERSONNEL AND EQUIPMENT OF THE HOSPITAL
    CORPS. 1887-1902. 31 vols. 2 ft.   119
    Volumes arranged alphabetically by name of post; returns arranged
chronologically by date of return.

REGISTER SHOWING GAINS AND LOSSES OF HOSPITAL CORPS NONCOMMISSIONED
    OFFICERS. 1887-1914. 1 vol. 1 in.   120
    Entries arranged chronologically by date of entrance into service.

REGISTERS SHOWING GAINS AND LOSSES OF HOSPITAL CORPS PERSONNEL.
    1889-1903. 8 vols. 1 ft.   <u>121</u>
    Arranged by period. Entries in each volume arranged by position
and thereunder chronologically by date of entrance on or separation
from service.

SUBJECT INDEX TO WAR DEPARTMENT AND SURGEON GENERAL'S ORDERS AND
    CIRCULARS (1887-94) PERTAINING TO HOSPITAL CORPS PERSONNEL. 1 vol.
    1/2 in.   <u>122</u>

2. Volunteer and Reserve Officers

a. Volunteer Medical Officers

LIST OF CANDIDATES SEEKING SERVICE WITH U.S. COLORED TROOPS AND WITH
    U.S. VOLUNTEERS. Apr. 1864-Apr. 1865. 1 vol. 1/2 in.   <u>123</u>
    Arranged chronologically by date of application.

REPORTS OF RESULTS OF EXAMINATIONS OF CANDIDATES SEEKING APPOINTMENT
    AS SURGEONS WITH U.S. VOLUNTEERS ("MERIT ROLLS"). 1861-65.
    2 vols. 2 in.   <u>124</u>
    Reports in each volume arranged chronologically by date Army
examining board was convened. There is much duplication in the
two volumes.

LIST OF VOLUNTEER MEDICAL OFFICERS WHO SERVED WITH CIVIL WAR ARMY
    CORPS. 1861-65. 25 pamphlets. 2 in.   <u>125</u>
    Arranged numerically by Army corps and thereunder by initial
letter of medical officer's name.

REGISTER OF VOLUNTEER MEDICAL OFFICERS ARRIVING AT THE SURGEON
    GENERAL'S OFFICE. Sept. 1862-Jan. 1867. 1 vol. 1 in.   <u>126</u>
    Entries arranged chronologically by date of officer's arrival.

STATEMENTS OF SERVICE OF CIVIL WAR MEDICAL CADETS. 1862-65. 3 in. <u>127</u>
    Arranged alphabetically by name of cadet.

REGISTER OF DEATHS OF CIVIL WAR VOLUNTEER MEDICAL OFFICERS. 1863-96.
    1 vol. 2 in.   <u>128</u>
    Arranged alphabetically by initial letter of officer's surname.
Includes deaths of Regular Army officers; for supplementary information see series 100.

ROSTERS OF REGIMENTAL MEDICAL OFFICERS, U.S. VOLUNTEERS, SPANISH-
    AMERICAN WAR. 1898-1901. 6 in.   <u>129</u>
    Two sets of cards, each arranged alphabetically by the home State
of the volunteer unit and thereunder by unit. Entries arranged chronologically by period of service with the unit.

REGISTER OF VOLUNTEER MEDICAL OFFICERS WHO SERVED IN THE PHILIPPINE
ISLANDS. 1898-1902. 1 vol. 1 in.   130
Arranged alphabetically by initial letter of surname of officer.

b. Medical Reserve Officers

REPORTS, LISTS, AND CORRESPONDENCE RELATING TO THE EXAMINATION AND
APPOINTMENT OF CANDIDATES TO THE MEDICAL RESERVE CORPS. 1908-10.
3 in.   131
Unarranged.

STATISTICAL DATA CARDS OF CANDIDATES SEEKING APPOINTMENT TO THE
MEDICAL RESERVE CORPS AND TO THE MEDICAL OFFICERS RESERVE CORPS.
1908-18. 12 ft.   132
Arranged alphabetically by name of candidate.

PERSONAL DATA CARDS OF MEMBERS OF THE MEDICAL RESERVE CORPS AND OF
THE MEDICAL OFFICERS RESERVE CORPS. 1908-17. 6 ft.   133
Arranged alphabetically by name of officer.

c. Dental Reserve Officers

PERSONAL DATA CARDS OF CANDIDATES SEEKING APPOINTMENT TO THE DENTAL
RESERVE CORPS. 1917-18. 2 ft.   134
Arranged alphabetically by name in two subseries: persons
appointed and persons not appointed.

d. National Guard Medical and Dental Officers

ROSTERS OF MEDICAL OFFICERS AND HOSPITAL CORPS ORGANIZATIONS OF THE
NATIONAL GUARD. 1896-98. 1 vol. 1 in.   135
Grouped under names of States. Includes an alphabetical index
to States.

PERSONAL HISTORY CARDS OF MEDICAL AND DENTAL OFFICERS OF THE NATIONAL
GUARD. 1915-17. 1 ft.   136
Arranged in two subseries (medical and dental officers), thereunder alphabetically by State, and thereunder alphabetically by name
of officer.

G. Records Relating to Civilian Personnel, 1862-1939

1. Contract (Acting Assistant) Surgeons

PERSONAL DATA CARDS OF CIVIL WAR CONTRACT SURGEONS. 1862-1914.
1 ft.   137
Arranged alphabetically by name (A-L).

REGISTERS SHOWING SERVICE OF CONTRACT SURGEONS. 1898-1914. 4 vols.
7 in.   138
    Arranged chronologically by date of contract. For registers of
military service of contract surgeons for the period 1876-79 see
series 90.

SERVICE HISTORY CARDS OF CONTRACT SURGEONS. 1898-1915. 10 in.   139
    Arranged alphabetically by name.

LIST OF CONTRACT SURGEONS SERVING WITH CAVALRY AND INFANTRY REGIMENTS.
1866-91. 1/4 in.   140
    Arranged by arm of service, thereunder numerically by regiment
number, and thereunder chronologically by date of contract.

ROSTERS OF CONTRACT SURGEONS ON DUTY WITH REGULAR ARMY UNITS.
1898-1903. 5 in.   141
    Arranged alphabetically by arm of service, and thereunder
numerically by unit number. Entries under units are in no dis-
cernible order.

REPORTS OF CONTRACT SURGEONS CONCERNING THEIR PREVIOUS SERVICE WITH
THE MEDICAL DEPARTMENT. 1875-82. 1 vol. 1/2 in.   142
    Arranged by initial letter of surname of surgeon and thereunder
chronologically by date of report.

MONTHLY RETURNS OF CONTRACT SURGEONS SERVING IN MILITARY DEPARTMENTS.
1888-92. 4 in.   143
    Arranged by year, thereunder by military department, and there-
under by month.

REGISTER OF CONTRACT SURGEONS CONSIDERED UNFIT FOR REEMPLOYMENT
("BLACK LIST"). 1864-80. 1 vol. 1/2 in.   144
    Arranged alphabetically by initial letter of surname of contract
surgeon and thereunder chronologically by date of entry.

2. Contract (Acting) Dental Surgeons

SERVICE DATA CARDS OF CONTRACT DENTISTS WHO WERE COMMISSIONED DENTAL
SURGEONS IN 1911. 1901-11. 1/4 in.   145
    Arranged alphabetically by name of officer.

SUMMARY DATA CARDS SHOWING THE SERVICE HISTORY OF CONTRACT DENTAL
SURGEONS. 1911-16. 1 in.   146
    Arranged alphabetically by name of surgeon.

3.c Contract Nurses

For records relating to Regular Army Nurses (1901-51),
see series 103-109.

CORRESPONDENCE RELATING TO SPANISH-AMERICAN WAR CONTRACT NURSES.
    1898-1910. 2 ft.   147
    Unarranged.

REGISTERS OF SERVICE OF SPANISH-AMERICAN WAR CONTRACT NURSES.
    1898-1900. 8 vols. 2 ft.   148
    Entries arranged chronologically by date of contract. Each
volume has a name index. Volumes are mislabeled "Record of Military
History of Post."

PERSONAL DATA CARDS OF SPANISH-AMERICAN WAR CONTRACT NURSES.
    1898-1939. 6 ft.   149
    Arranged alphabetically by name.

CORRESPONDENCE RELATING TO THE SERVICE OF SPANISH-AMERICAN WAR
    CONTRACT NURSES. 1898-1939. 6 ft.   150
    Arranged alphabetically by name of nurse.

4. Clerks and Laborers

LIST OF CLERKS, GENERAL SERVICE MEN, LABORERS, AND WATCHMEN IN THE
    SURGEON GENERAL'S OFFICE. July 1878. 1 vol. 1/2 in.   151
    Grouped by position and thereunder either alphabetically by name
or by grade.

REGISTER SHOWING APPOINTMENTS, PROMOTIONS, TRANSFERS, LEAVES OF
    ABSENCE, AND RESIGNATIONS OF CLERKS IN THE SURGEON GENERAL'S
    OFFICE. 1887-89. 1 vol. 1 in.   152
    Entries grouped by subject and arranged thereunder chronologically
by date of action.

REGISTER OF CIVILIAN EMPLOYEES OF THE SURGEON GENERAL'S OFFICE AND
    OF THE MEDICAL SUPPLY DEPOTS. 1891-97. 1 vol. 1/2 in.   153
    Entries arranged by place of employment, thereunder chronologically
by year, and thereunder by grade or name of employee.

REGISTER OF CIVILIAN EMPLOYEES IN THE FIELD OFFICES OF THE MEDICAL
    DEPARTMENT. 1865-1904. 1 vol. 1 in.   154
    Entries arranged by field office and thereunder chronologically
by date of entry into service. Index to names of employees.

PERSONAL DATA CARDS OF CLASSIFIED EMPLOYEES IN THE MEDICAL DEPART-
    MENT. 1903-14. 4 in.   155
    Arranged alphabetically by name of employee.

5. Matrons, Cooks, and Laundresses

LIST OF FEMALE NURSES, COOKS, AND LAUNDRESSES EMPLOYED IN ARMY
    HOSPITALS DURING THE CIVIL WAR. n.d. 1 vol. 1/2 in.   156
    Arranged by locality, thereunder by hospital, and thereunder
alphabetically by name.

REGISTER SHOWING GAINS AND LOSSES OF HOSPITAL MATRONS ON DUTY AT
    ARMY POSTS. Jan. 1893-Nov. 1904. 1 vol. 1/2 in.   .157
    Entries arranged chronologically by date of entrance on or
separation from duty.

H. Records Relating to Fiscal Matters, 1822-1928

1. Estimates

ANNUAL ESTIMATES. 1871-87. 1 vol. 1 in.   158
    Arranged chronologically. Subject index.

ANNUAL ESTIMATES. 1886-90. 5 in.   159
    Arranged by year.

ESTIMATES APPROVED BY THE SECRETARY OF WAR FOR THE CONSTRUCTION AND
    REPAIR OF POST HOSPITALS. 1872-75. 1 vol. 1 in.   160
    Arranged chronologically.

ANNUAL SUMMARY REPORTS OF ESTIMATES AND DISBURSEMENTS ON ACCOUNT OF
    THE APPROPRIATION FOR CONSTRUCTION AND REPAIR OF HOSPITALS.
    1895-1918. 1 vol. 1 in.   161
    Arranged by fiscal year and thereunder by military department.

APPROVED ESTIMATES FOR CONSTRUCTION AND REPAIR OF HOSPITAL STEWARDS'
    QUARTERS. 1889-1912. 1 vol. 1/2 in.   162
    Arranged by fiscal year.

2. Requisitions for Funds

REGISTER OF REQUISITIONS ON THE SECRETARY OF WAR FOR FUNDS. Dec. 1864-
    June 1869. 1 vol. 1 in.   163
    Arranged chronologically.

REQUISITIONS ON THE SECRETARY OF WAR FOR FUNDS. 1836-71. 5 vols.
    7 in.   164
    Arranged chronologically. Volumes 2-5 have name indexes. For
a register to parts of volumes 4 and 5 see series 163.

REQUESTS FOR TREASURY WARRANTS. 1896-1917. 3 vols. 3 in.   165
    Arranged chronologically. There is a name index in each volume.

3. Disbursements

NAME INDEX TO LEDGERS A-F OF SERIES 167 AND IN DAYBOOKS NUMBERED 3-5 OF SERIES 195. 1822-62. 1 vol. 1 in.   166
    The index is to disbursing officers named in the ledgers and to disbursing officers and claimants named in the daybooks.

LEDGERS OF DISBURSEMENTS ON ACCOUNT OF VARIOUS MEDICAL DEPARTMENT APPROPRIATIONS. (LEDGERS A-G). 1824-63. 7 vols. 1 ft.   167
    Entries in volume arranged by appropriation and thereunder chronologically. For name index to ledgers A-F see series 166.

LEDGER OF DISBURSEMENTS ON ACCOUNT OF VARIOUS MEDICAL DEPARTMENT APPROPRIATIONS. 1906-17. 1 vol. 3 in.   168
    Arranged by appropriation and thereunder chronologically by fiscal year.

LEDGERS OF DISBURSEMENTS BY MEDICAL OFFICERS FOR NONMEDICAL EXPENDITURES ("MISCELLANEOUS ACCOUNTS"). 1862-78. 2 vols. 3 in.   169
    Arranged chronologically and thereunder by name of disbursing officer. Name and subject index in each volume.

LEDGER OF DISBURSEMENTS ON ACCOUNT OF THE PRISONER-OF-WAR APPROPRIATION. 1863-65. 1 vol. 2 in.   170
    Entries grouped by name of disbursing officer. Name index.

NAME INDEX TO VOLUME 2 OF SERIES 172. 1866-69. 1 vol. 1/2 in.   171

STATEMENTS OF EXPENDITURES ON ACCOUNT OF THE CONTINGENT FUND. 1863-81. 2 vols. 2 in.   172
    Arranged chronologically. For a name index to volume 2 see series 171.

REGISTERS OF DISBURSEMENTS ON ACCOUNT OF THE MEDICAL AND HOSPITAL DEPARTMENT APPROPRIATION. 1875-1905. 2 vols. 4 in.   173
    Arranged chronologically by fiscal year. Similar disbursements for a later period are recorded in series 168.

REGISTERS OF DISBURSEMENTS ON ACCOUNT OF APPROPRIATIONS FOR CONSTRUCTION AND REPAIR OF HOSPITALS. 1875-1928. 6 vols. 7 in.   174
    Arranged chronologically.

TABULATED STATEMENTS OF ALLOTMENTS FOR CONSTRUCTION AND REPAIR OF HOSPITALS. 1875-1902. 1 vol. 1 in.   175
    Grouped by post or station. Index to names of stations.

REGISTER OF EXPENDITURES FOR CONSTRUCTION AND REPAIR OF HOSPITAL
    STEWARDS' QUARTERS. 1887-1918. 2 vols. 1 in.   176
    Arranged chronologically by fiscal year and thereunder by
military department.

REGISTER OF DISBURSEMENTS ON ACCOUNT OF THE ARMY MEDICAL MUSEUM AND
    LIBRARY APPROPRIATIONS. 1889-1906. 1 vol. 2 in.   177
    Arranged chronologically by fiscal year. Similar disbursements
for a later period are recorded in series 168.

REGISTER OF AUTHORIZATIONS FOR PURCHASES AT ARMY POSTS AND BY ARMY
    COMMANDS. 1910-14. 1 vol. 1 in.   178
    Arranged chronologically.

REGISTER OF DISBURSEMENTS REQUIRING THE APPROVAL OF THE SURGEON
    GENERAL. 1913-17. 1 vol. 3 in.   179
    Entries grouped under three subheadings ("Contracts and reserve,"
"Army posts," and "Medical depots"), and arranged thereunder chronologically.

NAME INDEXES TO DISBURSING OFFICERS NAMED IN PART OF SERIES 181.
    4 vols. 5 in.   180

ABSTRACTS OF DISBURSEMENTS MADE BY MEDICAL OFFICERS. 1862-1916.
    87 vols. 18 ft.   181
    Entries in each volume grouped by disbursing officer and there-
under by appropriation; under the latter they are arranged chronologically. The later volumes have name indexes. For name indexes
to the early volumes see series 180.

SUMMARY ACCOUNTS OF DISBURSEMENTS MADE BY MEDICAL OFFICERS (LEDGERS
    E, H, AND H1). 1822-83; 1898-1914. 3 vols. 9 in.   182
    Grouped by name of disbursing officer and arranged thereunder
chronologically.

SCHEDULE OF PAYMENTS MADE BY ARMY PAYMASTERS TO CONTRACT SURGEONS
    AND EMPLOYEES UNDER THEIR SUPERVISION. 1864-70. 1 vol. 1 in. 183
    Grouped by paymaster and arranged thereunder chronologically.
Name index to payees.

       4. Money Accounts

MONTHLY STATEMENTS OF FUNDS RECEIVED AND DISBURSEMENTS MADE BY THE
    MEDICAL DEPARTMENT. 1880-89. 1 vol. 1 in.   184
    Arranged chronologically by month.

MONEY ACCOUNTS OF THE DISBURSING OFFICER OF THE MEDICAL DEPARTMENT.
    1906-9. 11 vols. 2 ft.   185
    Arranged chronologically by month.

MONTHLY SUMMARY OF ACCOUNTS OF DISBURSING OFFICERS. 1899-1902.
    1 vol. 1/4 in.   186
    Arranged chronologically. Name index to disbursing officers.

MONTHLY STATEMENTS OF ACCOUNT CURRENT OF MEDICAL DEPARTMENT DIS-
    BURSING OFFICERS. 1907-16. 1 vol. 3 in.   187
    Grouped by station of disbursing officer and arranged thereunder
chronologically.

ACCOUNTS OF MEDICAL PURVEYORS. 1864-67. 1 vol. 2 in.   188
    Grouped by name of medical purveyor and thereunder by appropria-
tion. Indexed by name.

ABSTRACTS OF CORRESPONDENCE RELATING TO ACCOUNTS OF ASSISTANT SURGEONS.
    1865-68. 2 vols. 3 in.   189
    Arranged chronologically. Indexed by name of officer.

REGISTER SHOWING THE SETTLEMENT OF ACCOUNTS OF CONTRACT SURGEONS.
    1865-1901. 1 vol. 3 in.   190
    Arranged alphabetically by initial letter of contract surgeon's
name and thereunder chronologically.

CASH BOOK OF COL. THOMAS U. RAYMOND, MEDICAL CORPS PURCHASING
    OFFICER, LONDON, ENGLAND. 1918-19. 1 vol. 3 in.   191
    Entries arranged chronologically.

LEDGERS OF ACCOUNTS WITH THE UNITED STATES TREASURY (LEDGERS D AND D2).
    1849-1906. 2 vols. 5 in.   192
    Entries arranged chronologically to 1870; after 1870 arranged by
type of appropriation and thereunder chronologically.

REGISTER OF THE SECOND AUDITOR'S STATEMENTS OF DIFFERENCES IN ACCOUNTS
    OF MEDICAL OFFICERS. 1863-1908. 1 vol. 2 in.   193
    Grouped by name of officer. Index to names.

5. Individual Claims and Accounts

NAME INDEXES TO VOLUMES NUMBERED 7-15 OF SERIES 195. 2 vols.
    3 in.   194

DAYBOOKS OF APPROVED ACCOUNTS AND CLAIMS SENT TO THE TREASURY DEPART-
    MENT FOR SETTLEMENT. 1822-1900. 14 vols. 4 ft.   195
    Entries in each volume are arranged chronologically. Some volumes
contain name indexes to claimants. For indexes to disbursing officers

or claimants named in volumes numbered 3-5 and 7-15, see series 166 and 194 respectively.

REGISTERS OF CLAIMS SETTLED BY THE SECOND AUDITOR OF THE TREASURY DEPARTMENT (DAYBOOKS A1 AND A2). 1849-64. 2 vols. 3 in.   **196**
   Arranged chronologically. Both volumes have name indexes.

REGISTERS OF ACCOUNTS AND CLAIMS REFERRED TO SOME OTHER OFFICER OR DEPARTMENT FOR APPROVAL ("REFERRED ACCOUNTS"). 1863-1914. 8 vols.   **197**
(Nos. 1-8). 2 ft.
   Entries in each volume are grouped by appropriation and arranged thereunder chronologically. There is a name index in each volume.

REGISTERS OF ACCOUNTS AND CLAIMS APPROVED BY THE SURGEON GENERAL AND REFERRED FOR PAYMENT ("REFERRED ACCOUNTS"). 1885-1913. 7 vols.   **198**
(Nos. 9-15). 1 ft.
   Arranged by fiscal year, thereunder by appropriation, and thereunder chronologically.

REGISTERS OF APPROVED CLAIMS FOR SERVICES AND SUPPLIES. Feb. 1883-July 1909. 11 vols. 2 ft.   **199**
   Arranged chronologically by date claim was received. Each volume has a name index. Some volumes are labeled "Miscellaneous Bills" or "Record of Military History of Post.")

REGISTER SHOWING CHARGES FOR SERVICES OF PRIVATE PHYSICIANS. 1886-88. 1 vol. 1 in.   **200**
   Entries grouped by station. Name index.

NAME INDEX TO PHYSICIANS NAMED IN SERIES 202. 6 in.   **201**
   Card index.

CLAIMS OF PHYSICIANS FOR MEDICAL ATTENDANCE ON MILITARY PERSONNEL. 1898-1900. 12 ft.   **202**
   These claims are enclosures to letters received by the Surgeon General. They are arranged by file number as in series 26. Name index in series 201.

CLAIMS IN CIVILIAN HOSPITALS FOR MEDICAL ATTENDANCE ON MILITARY PERSONNEL. 1898-1900. 1 ft.   **203**
   Arranged alphabetically by State (Alabama to New York only) and thereunder numerically by assigned number.

CLAIMS OF VERMONT SOLDIERS FOR PAYMENT OF MEDICAL EXPENSES. 1898-1900.   **204**
2 ft.
   Arranged alphabetically by name of claimant.

6. Contracts

For contracts of the Property Division (1884-94), the Hospital Corps and Supply Division (1894-99), and the Supply Division (1899-1913), see series 275.

LIST OF CONTRACTS ON ACCOUNT OF THE MEDICAL DEPARTMENT.
See volume 3 of series 76.

REGISTER OF CONTRACTS WITH CIVILIAN SURGEONS. 1871-85. 1 vol. 1/4 in.   <u>205</u>
Arranged chronologically by date of contract.

REGISTER OF CONTRACTS ON ACCOUNT OF THE MEDICAL AND HOSPITAL DIVISION APPROPRIATION. 1907-14. 1 vol. 1 in.   <u>206</u>
Arranged chronologically by date of contract.

I.   Records Relating to Medical Property and Supplies, 1818-1925

1.   Property Returns

REGISTERS OF MEDICAL AND HOSPITAL PROPERTY RETURNS. 1818-65. 4 vols. 6 in.   <u>207</u>
Entries in each volume arranged alphabetically by initial letter of medical officer's surname and thereunder chronologically by date of receipt of return.

ABSTRACTS OF MEDICAL AND HOSPITAL PROPERTY RETURNS. 1858-66. 1 vol. 2 in.   <u>208</u>
Arranged chronologically by year within three subseries: posts, medical officers, and Territorial commands.

REGISTER OF SCHEDULES OF MEDICAL AND HOSPITAL PROPERTY RETURNS EXAMINED AND SENT TO THE SECOND AUDITOR. 1861-1903. 1 vol. 4 in.   <u>209</u>
Arranged by schedule number or letter and thereunder alphabetically by initial letter of surname of officer making the return.

REGISTER OF DURABLE PROPERTY RETURNS. 1873-78. 1 vol. 1 in.   <u>210</u>
Arranged alphabetically by initial letter of submitting officer's name.

CONSOLIDATED ABSTRACTS OF MEDICAL AND HOSPITAL PROPERTY ISSUED TO POSTS. 1874-80. 2 vols. 2 in.   <u>211</u>
Arranged by year.

2. Sales and Transfers

REGISTER OF SALES OF MEDICAL DEPARTMENT PROPERTY. 1871-1913.
   1 vol. 1 in.
   Arranged chronologically.
212

REGISTERS OF MEDICAL SUPPLIES ISSUED TO STATES, SOLD TO STATES, OR
   TRANSFERRED TO OTHER BRANCHES OF THE FEDERAL GOVERNMENT. 1902-17.
   2 vols. 2 in.
   Arranged chronologically.
213

REGISTER SHOWING THE DISPOSITION OF SURPLUS MEDICAL PROPERTY.
   1921-23. 1 vol. 1/4 in.
   Arranged chronologically.
214

SEMIMONTHLY REPORTS OF SURPLUS PROPERTY ACTIVITIES. Jan. 1921-
   Mar. 1924. 1 vol. 1/4 in.
   Arranged chronologically.
215

SEMIMONTHLY REPORTS TO THE DIRECTOR OF SALES CONCERNING THE DISPOSITION
   OF SURPLUS PROPERTY. July 1922-Oct. 1925. 1 vol. 1/4 in.
   Arranged chronologically.
216

3. Miscellaneous

REGISTER OF ARTICLES RECEIVED IN THE STOREHOUSE. Aug. 1846-Mar. 1847.
   1 vol. 1 in.
   Arranged chronologically.
217

INVOICES OF MEDICAL STORES. 1863-70. 4 vols. 10 in.
   Arranged chronologically. Name index in each volume.
218

J. Records Relating to Hospitals, 1861-1927

REGISTERS OF ARMY HOSPITALS AND THEIR STAFFS. 1861-70. 2 vols.
   4 in.
   Arranged alphabetically by name of hospital. There are entries
for a few hospitals as late as 1893.
219

LISTS OF ARMY GENERAL HOSPITALS IN OPERATION DURING THE CIVIL WAR.
   1861-66. 2 vols. 1/4 in.
   Arranged by State.
220

MONTHLY LISTS OF ARMY GENERAL AND POST HOSPITALS IN THE UNITED STATES.
   1863-67. 2 in.
   Arranged chronologically.
221

REGISTERS OF CONSTRUCTION OF AND REPAIRS TO POST HOSPITALS AND OTHER
  MEDICAL FACILITIES. 1875-1917. 2 vols. 3 in.   222
    Entries in each volume grouped by post and arranged thereunder
chronologically. Name index to posts in each volume.

ABSTRACTS OF CORRESPONDENCE AND ORDERS RELATING TO THE ESTABLISHMENT
  AND ORGANIZATION OF THE ARMY AND NAVY GENERAL HOSPITAL, HOT SPRINGS,
  ARK. 1882-88. 1 vol. 1 in.   223
    Arranged chronologically. Name and subject index included.

REGISTER OF HOSPITAL CONSTRUCTION PROJECTS. 1919-26. 1 vol.
  2 in.   224
    Entries grouped by post and arranged thereunder chronologically.

STATISTICAL CHARTS AND TABLES RELATING TO COMPLETED AND PROPOSED
  HOSPITAL CONSTRUCTION PROJECTS. 1922-27. 1/4 in.   225
    Arranged chronologically.

  K.   Records of Individual Medical Department Officers, 1820-1936

LETTERS SENT BY SURGEON THOMAS LAWSON. Apr. 1820-July 1822; Oct. 1825.
  1 vol. 1 in.   226
    Arranged chronologically.

LETTER BOOK OF SURGEON THOMAS F. AZPELL. 1862-76. 1 vol. 1 in.   227
    Arranged chronologically.

LETTERS RECEIVED BY SURGEON LINCOLN R. STONE, U.S. VOLUNTEERS, IN
  CHARGE OF THE GENERAL HOSPITAL AT GALLIPOLIS, OHIO. 1864. 1 vol.
  1 in.   228
    Unarranged.

JOURNAL OF DR. ANITA NEWCOMB McGEE. 1898-99. 2 vols. 2 in.   229
    Arranged chronologically.

CORRESPONDENCE OF DR. ANITA NEWCOMB McGEE. 1898-1936. 2 ft.   230
    Unarranged.

PAPERS OF COL. J. R. KEAN AND COL. W. J. LYSTER. 1905-16. 1 ft.   231
    Arranged by subject in two alphabetical files, with some papers
of Kean unarranged.

  L.   Reference Aids, 1790-1948

    Many of the series under this heading were created as a result
of the provision contained in the Instructions For Keeping the Records
And Transacting the Clerical Business of the War Department (1870) that

"Memorandum Books, simple in design and inexpensive in character, may be used to aid in the dispatch of current business or for ready reference to particular classes of information."

ABSTRACTS OF U.S. STATUTES AND ARMY REGULATIONS RELATING TO THE MEDICAL DEPARTMENT (1790-1898). 2 in. 232
Arranged chronologically.

LISTS OF COMMANDS AND STATIONS COMPRISING CIVIL WAR MILITARY DEPART-MENTS. 1861-66. 1 vol. 1/2 in. 233
Arranged by list number (1-27).

REFERENCE BOOK TO LETTERS RECEIVED, 1861-70 ("INDEX TO LETTERS FILED, SURGEON GENERAL'S OFFICE"). 1 vol. 2 in. 234
Name and subject entries arranged alphabetically (L-Z).

DECISIONS OF GOVERNMENT OFFICIALS RELATING TO THE SURGEON GENERAL'S OFFICE. 1866-92. 1 vol. 2 in. 235
Arranged chronologically. Subject index.

NAME AND SUBJECT INDEXES ("REFERENCE BOOKS") TO IMPORTANT LETTERS IN PART (1871-89) OF SERIES 12. 2 vols. 1/2 in. 236

SUBJECT INDEX TO WAR DEPARTMENT DECISIONS CONCERNING MEDICAL OFFICERS IN PART (1871-89) OF SERIES 12. 1 vol. 1/4 in. 237

ABSTRACTS OF DECISIONS OF THE WAR DEPARTMENT RELATING TO CONTRACT SURGEONS (1872-86). 1 vol. 1 in. 238
Arranged chronologically. Subject index. Included are a few forms and form letters.

SUBJECT INDEX TO VARIOUS ITEMS OF WAR DEPARTMENT AND SURGEON GENERAL'S OFFICE INFORMATION ("POLICY AND PRECEDENT BOOK"). 1871-89. 1 vol. 239
1/2 in.

REFERENCE FILE ("POLICY AND PRECEDENT FILE"). 1887-1948. 36 ft. 240
Chiefly copies of correspondence, issuances, and reference cards. Arranged alphabetically by subject and thereunder chronologically.

"MEMORANDUM BOOK" RELATING TO THE HOSPITAL CORPS. 1887-1905. 241
1 vol. 1 in.
Arranged chronologically.

DECISIONS AND OPINIONS OF THE JUDGE ADVOCATE GENERAL RELATING TO THE MEDICAL DEPARTMENT. 1904-9. 3 in. 242
Arranged alphabetically by subject.

CLIPPINGS FROM MEDICAL JOURNALS AND NEWSPAPERS RELATING TO THE
  MEDICAL DEPARTMENT. 1904-19. 2 vols. 5 in.   <u>243</u>
  Arranged chronologically.

   M. <u>Miscellaneous Records, 1816-1919</u>

"ORDERS FROM THE SECRETARY OF WAR, FORMS, AND RESOLUTIONS OF CONGRESS.
  June 1816-Dec. 1837. 2 vols. 3 in.   <u>244</u>
  Arranged chronologically. Volume 1 has a name and subject index.

MISCELLANEOUS RECORDS, CHIEF CLERK'S OFFICE. ca. 1880-1917. 2 ft.   <u>245</u>
  Unarranged.

REPLIES TO QUESTIONNAIRES REGARDING PROPOSED REVISION OF THE MEDICAL
  INSPECTION FORM. 1891. 3 in.   <u>246</u>
  Unarranged.

PLANS OF MILITARY POSTS IN THE PHILIPPINE ISLANDS. 1905. 1 vol.
  1/4 in.   <u>247</u>
  Arranged alphabetically by name of post.

QUESTIONNAIRES AND REPORTS RELATING TO A PROPOSED VETERINARY HISTORY
  OF WORLD WAR I. 1918-19. 5 ft.   <u>248</u>
  Arranged alphabetically by installation.

CHARTS SHOWING ORGANIZATION AND ACTIVITIES OF THE MEDICAL DEPARTMENT.
  Jan. 1918. 1 vol. 1/2 in.   <u>249</u>

UNIDENTIFIED NAME INDEX (CA. 1870). 1 vol. 1/2 in.   <u>250</u>

UNIDENTIFIED NAME INDEX (CA. 1880). 1 vol. 1/4 in.   <u>251</u>

NAME AND SUBJECT INDEX TO "CORRESPONDENCE SENT-B" (1898). 1 vol.
  1/2 in.   <u>252</u>
  Correspondence not found.

UNIDENTIFIED LIST OF MALE AND FEMALE NAMES. 1 vol. 1/4 in.   <u>253</u>
  Arranged alphabetically.

II. <u>Subordinate Offices</u>

   A. <u>Finance Division, 1873-91</u>

     The Finance Division examined and kept the money accounts of
the Medical Department from the time of the Civil War until 1893. In
addition, this division was responsible for carrying out the provisions

of an act of June 17, 1870, granting commutation for artificial limbs and appliances to disabled Union soldiers. This latter function was transferred to the Disbursing Division in November 1888, and in June 1893, the remaining functions of the Finance Division were given to the Administrative Division.

LETTERS SENT. July 1873-Sept. 1885. 2 vols. 4 in.   254
    Arranged chronologically. Each volume has a name index. Volume 1 is labeled "Division of Accounts."

NAME INDEX TO SERIES 256. 1 vol. 1 in.   255

REGISTER OF LETTERS RECEIVED. 1873-91. 1 vol. 2 in.   256
    Arranged chronologically. Volume is labeled "Division of Accounts." For an index see series 255.

    B. _Property Division, 1873-94_

    An order of the Surgeon General, dated April 20, 1874, formally established the Property Division and placed Chief Medical Purveyor J. H. Baxter at its head. The duties of this division included the purchase and distribution of medical supplies, the settlement of property returns, and the examination of certain accounts of medical disbursing officers. Most of these duties were taken over by the Hospital Corps and Supply Division when the Property Division was discontinued on June 30, 1894.

NAME AND SUBJECT INDEXES TO SERIES 258. 16 vols. 1 ft.   257
    Annual indexes.

LETTERS SENT. 1874-89. 18 vols. 6 ft.   258
    Arranged chronologically. There is a name and subject index in each volume. For other name and subject indexes see series 257.

NAME AND SUBJECT INDEXES TO SERIES 260. 16 vols. 1 ft.   259
    Annual indexes.

REGISTERS OF LETTERS RECEIVED. 1874-89. 20 vols. 6 ft.   260
    Arranged chronologically by year. The entries in each volume are numbered consecutively. For name and subject indexes see series 259.

NAME AND SUBJECT INDEXES TO SERIES 262. 16 vols. 1 ft.   261
    Annual indexes.

ENDORSEMENTS. 1874; 1877-89. 14 vols. 3 ft.   262
    Arranged chronologically. Each volume contains a name and subject index. For other name and subject indexes see series 261.

REGISTER OF RECORD CARDS FOR GENERAL CORRESPONDENCE. Jan. 1890-
    June 1894. 1 vol. 2 in.   263
        Arranged chronologically by year and thereunder numerically by
file number.

RECORD CARDS FOR GENERAL CORRESPONDENCE. 1891-92. 2 ft.   264
        Arranged by subject, thereunder by name or additional subject,
and thereunder by file number of correspondence. The correspondence
to which these refer has not been found. For register see series 263.

LETTERS AND ENDORSEMENTS SENT BY THE CHIEF MEDICAL PURVEYOR. On.
    Oct. 1873-Feb. 1874. 1 vol. 1 in.   265
        Arranged chronologically.

SEMIOFFICIAL LETTERS SENT BY THE CHIEF MEDICAL PURVEYOR. 1881-90;
    1893-94. 3 vols. 3 in.   266
        Arranged chronologically. Each volume has a name and subject
index.

REGISTER OF LETTERS RECEIVED BY THE CHIEF MEDICAL PURVEYOR. Oct.
    Oct. 1873-Mar. 1874. 1 vol. 1 in.   267
        Arranged chronologically. The entries are numbered consecutively.
The volume contains a name and subject index.

    C. Finance and Supply Division, 1883-1918

        On September 20, 1917, by an order of the Surgeon General,
this division was created by a consolidation of the Accounting Branch
and the Property Branch of the Record, Correspondence, and Examining
Division and the Purchasing and Distribution Branches of the Supply
Division. In 1918 certain functions of the division were assumed by
the Chemical Warfare Service, Finance Service, Motor Transport Corps,
and the Purchase, Storage, and Traffic Division of the General Staff.
Although almost all medical procurement was taken over by the last
agency, this function was returned to the Finance and Supply Division
in 1920, when the Purchase, Storage, and Traffic Division was discontinued.

        From 1920 to 1942 the division had administrative supervision
over Medical Department finance and supply, construction and repair of
hospitals, supply depots, and procurement planning. In March 1942 it
was redesignated the Finance Division.

LETTERS SENT AND RECEIVED BY THE MEDICAL DEPARTMENT DISBURSING
    OFFICERS. 1883-1918. 2 vols. 3 in.   268
        Arranged chronologically. Each volume has a name and subject
index.

D. Sanitary and Disbursing Division, 1884-1906

This division was created on July 2, 1894, to handle all business connected with the furnishing of trusses, appliances, and artificial limbs to disabled soldiers and to "examine, perfect, and file" a number of routine and special Medical Department reports. The transfer of the Personal Identity Section to the Adjutant General's Office in late 1903 considerably reduced the volume of the division's work. With the removal of the Disbursing Section to the Supply Division in January 1909, the Sanitary and Disbursing Division was redesignated the Sanitary Division.

1. General Records

LETTERS AND ENDORSEMENTS SENT REGARDING TRUSSES. July 1884-Aug. 1886; Aug. 1887-Feb. 1891; Jan. 1892-Dec. 1895. 7 vols. 8 in.   269
Arranged chronologically. Each volume has a name index.

2. Personal Identity Section

This section was established on December 21, 1892, and was attached to the Administrative Division. In June 1894 it became one of the three sections of the Sanitary and Disbursing Division and so remained until 1903, when it was transferred to the Adjutant General's Office.

The functions of the Personal Identity Section included the collection of data concerning the physical examination of recruits and the identification of recruits who had had prior service in the Army and of soldiers who were applying for pensions.

LETTERS AND ENDORSEMENTS SENT. 1892-93; 1900-1903. 3 vols. 3 in. 270
Arranged chronologically.

NAME INDEX TO VOLUMES 1 AND 2 OF SERIES 272. 1 vol. 1 in.   271

REGISTERS OF RECRUITS IDENTIFIED AND REPORTED TO THE ADJUTANT GENERAL. 272
1890-1905. 4 vols. 6 in.
Arranged chronologically by date of report to the Adjutant General. The entries are numbered consecutively. For an index to volumes 1 and 2 see series 271.

SUMMARY REPORTS CONCERNING THE IDENTIFICATION OF RECRUITS. 1890-273
1906. 1 vol. 1/2 in.
Arranged chronologically by date of report.

REGISTERS OF PHYSICAL DESCRIPTIONS OF DESERTERS. n.d. 2 vols. 274
3 in.
Arranged by color of eyes of deserter and thereunder by his height.

E. Supply Division, 1884-1913

The Supply Division was created by an order of Surgeon General George M. Sternberg dated January 16, 1899. It was responsible for the purchase and distribution of medical and hospital supplies to the Army and to the National Guard. On September 20, 1917, the division was combined with the Accounting Branch and the Property Branch of the Record, Correspondence, and Examining Division to form the Finance and Supply Division.

REGISTERS OF CONTRACTS. 1884-1913. 2 vols. 4 in.   275
   Arranged chronologically. Included are entries for contracts made by the Property Division, 1884-94. A subject index to contracted items in each volume.

F. Hospital Corps Division, 1894

The Hospital Corps Division came into existence on January 1, 1894, by an order of the Surgeon General dated December 22, 1893. On June 30, 1894, it was merged into a new division known as the Hospital Corps and Supply Division. This merger lasted until January 1899, when the Hospital Corps Division again became a separate office. On August 1, 1903, it became a section of the newly created Personnel Division.

REGISTER OF RECORD CARDS FOR GENERAL CORRESPONDENCE. Jan.-June 1894.
   1 vol. 2 in.   276
   Arranged numerically.

G. Personnel Division, 1906-15

The Personnel Division was established on August 1, 1903, by order of Surgeon General Robert M. O'Reilly. Its functions included the procurement, classification, assignment, promotion, and discharge of Medical Department personnel. In 1932 the Division's title was changed to Military Personnel Division.

SEMIOFFICIAL LETTER BOOKS OF OFFICERS IN CHARGE. Oct. 1906-Oct. 1909;
   May 1912-Sept. 1915. 7 vols. 1 ft.   277
   Arranged chronologically. Name index in each volume.

H. Organization Division, 1917-25

The Coordination, Organization, and Equipment Division was established by Office Order No. 451, dated August 8, 1919. The division was redesignated the Organization Division in October 1922. Its functions included the systematic study of Medical Department organization and equipment; the preparation or revision of all Medical Department service manuals and tables of organization; and the study, prior to publication, of all War Department issuances involving Medical Department policy. On July 1, 1925, the division became a subdivision of the newly created Planning and Training Division.

BACKGROUND PAPERS AND DRAFTS OF REVISIONS OF ARMY REGULATIONS PERTAINING TO THE MEDICAL DEPARTMENT. 1920-25. 2 ft.   278
    Unarranged.

BACKGROUND PAPERS AND DRAFTS OF WAR DEPARTMENT FORMS AND SPECIAL REGULATIONS PERTAINING TO THE MEDICAL DEPARTMENT. 1920-25.   279
5 in.
    Arranged by type of issuance and thereunder numerically.

MISCELLANEOUS RECORDS. 1917-25. 7 ft.   280
    Unarranged. Includes records of medical units of the American Expeditionary Forces.

I. Hospital Division, 1917-20; 1940

From 1939 to June 1943 hospital construction and hospital operations were supervised by separate divisions. In July 1943 they were merged into the Hospital Administrative Division, which was renamed the Hospital Division in 1944. This division established general policies governing hospitalization, reviewed construction plans, surveyed civilian medical facilities offered for Army use, computed hospital bed requirements, and cooperated with the Office of the Chief of Transportation on matters connected with hospital ships and hospital trains.

BLUEPRINTS OF HOSPITALS AND MEDICAL BUILDINGS, HOSPITAL CONSTRUCTION DIVISION. 1917-20; 1940-50. 6 ft.   281
    Unarranged.

LABORATORY REPORTS. 1942-50. 3 ft.   282
    Grouped by type of report.

J. Nursing Division, 1918-33; 1951

Until August 1942 this division was known as the Nursing Service. It formulated and supervised the application of professional policies governing the Army Nurse Corps and established procedures and furnished advice on the training of United States Cadet nurses.

RECORDS OF THE ARMY SCHOOL OF NURSING. 1918-33; 1951. 3 ft.   283
    Arranged by subject and thereunder generally chronologically.

K. Purchase Division, 1932-45

The Purchase Division, sometimes called the Procurement Division, had responsibility during World War II for the production of medical supplies and equipment, contract negotiation and termination, and salvage. It also assisted the Medical Department contractors on problems involving the Controlled Materials Plan, priorities, and labor.

1. General Records

TAX EXEMPTION CERTIFICATES. June 1932-Jan. 1942. 1 in.   284
   Arranged chronologically.

RECORDS RELATING TO RESEARCH IN AND THE DEVELOPMENT OF DRUGS, CHEMICALS, AND BIOLOGICALS. 1941-45. 1 ft.   285
   Arranged alphabetically by name of drug or chemical and thereunder chronologically.

SECURITY-CLASSIFIED RECORDS RELATING TO RESEARCH IN AND THE DEVELOPMENT OF DRUGS, CHEMICALS, AND BIOLOGICALS. 1941-43. 4 in.   286
   Arranged alphabetically by subject.

RECORDS RELATING TO SMALLER WAR PLANTS POLICY. 1942-45. 1 in.   287
   Arranged chronologically.

SECURITY-CLASSIFIED RECORDS RELATING TO THE CONTROLLED MATERIALS PLAN. 1943-45. 2 ft.   288
   Arranged by subject.

2. Procurement and Policy Section

CORRESPONDENCE. 1941-45. 5 in.   289
   Arranged by subject and thereunder chronologically.

3. Manpower and Labor Section

CORRESPONDENCE. 1942-45. 4 in.   290
   Arranged chronologically.

L. Medical Statistics Division, 1940-50

This staff unit, known before World War II as the Statistics Division and the Vital Records Division, had four branches: Individual Records, Health Reports, Selective Service, and Statistical Analysis.

STATISTICAL HEALTH REPORTS. 1940-50. 10 ft.   291
   Grouped by type of report and arranged thereunder generally chronologically.

M. Military Personnel Division, 1941-45

This division took over the functions of the Personnel Division in 1932. By 1944 it consisted of nine branches, and was responsible for the procurement, appointment, assignment, training, promotion, and discharge of Medical Department personnel.

SPECIAL ORDERS OF THE SURGEON GENERAL'S OFFICE. 1941-45. 2 ft.   292
Arranged chronologically by year and thereunder numerically.

RECORDS RELATING TO THE MEDICAL OFFICERS CANDIDATE SCHOOL, CARLISLE
BARRACKS, PA. Sept. 1941-Oct. 1945. 2 in.   293
Arranged chronologically. Included are special orders of the school.

N. International (Supply) Division, 1942-47

The Defense Aid Subdivision, established in the Finance and Supply Division in 1941, transferred to the Procurement Division in 1942, and renamed the International Division about August 1942, advised and assisted the Surgeon General and the Chief of the Supply Service on all matters relating to the lend-lease and reciprocal-aid programs.

GENERAL CORRESPONDENCE. 1942-47. 15 ft.   294
Arranged by subject and thereunder generally chronologically.

SECURITY-CLASSIFIED CORRESPONDENCE. 1942-47. 3 ft.   295
Arranged numerically (Nos. 11000-14374).

O. Legal Division, 1942-47

This division was established in November 1942 to provide general legal advisory services for the Surgeon General's Office and its field agencies. It advised on legislation, regulations, and directives bearing upon the Medical Department, drafted procurement directives, reviewed competitive and negotiated contracts, and served as counsel on price-adjustment cases involving renegotiated contracts.

ROYALTY ADJUSTMENT CASE FILES. 1942-47. 5 ft.   296
Arranged alphabetically by name of firm.

P. Technical Information Division, 1942-45

This division had responsibility for the public-relations activities of the Surgeon General's Office subject to the review of the War Department's Bureau of Public Relations.

RECORDS RELATING TO THE ORGANIZATION AND PROCEDURES OF THE SURGEON
    GENERAL'S OFFICE. 1942-43. 4 ft.   297
    Arranged by subject and thereunder chronologically.

RECORDS RELATING TO PERSONNEL. Apr.-May 1945. 4 in.   298
    Arranged chronologically.

    Q. Training Division, 1942-45

        This division formulated and directed all Medical Department
training policies, plans, and programs; conducted inspections of medical
training centers; and supervised generally the medical training agencies
in the United States.

MISCELLANEOUS REPORTS AND EXHIBITS. 1942-45. 3 in.   299
    Unarranged.

    R. Medical Consultants Division, 1942-47

        The Medical Consultants Division supervised the practice of
internal medicine in the Army from late 1944 through 1945. The
division consisted of four branches for general medicine, communicable
diseases, tuberculosis, and tropical diseases.

RECORDS RELATING TO REPATRIATED PRISONERS OF WAR. 1942-47. 8 ft.   300
    Arranged alphabetically by subject.

    S. Women's Health and Welfare Unit, Professional Administrative
            Service, 1942-44.

        Formerly known as the WAC Liaison Branch, this unit developed
policies and coordinated all activities relating to the medical care
and welfare of women in the Army during World War II.

RECORDS RELATING TO THE PREPARATION OF FIELD MANUAL 35-20. 1942-44.
    1 ft.   301
    Arranged by subject.

    T. Inspection Branch, Mobilization and Overseas Operations
            Division, 1943-45

        This branch of the Mobilization and Overseas Operations
Division maintained records of overseas inspections by personnel of
the Surgeon General's Office during World War II, interviewed military
and civilian experts on medical and sanitary matters on their return
from overseas, and prepared reports on their findings.

INTERVIEWS WITH OFFICERS VISITING INSTALLATIONS OF THE SURGEON GENERAL'S
OFFICE. 1943-45. 3 ft.   302
Arranged numerically by number of interview.

TEMPORARY DUTY REPORTS. Nov. 1943-May 1945. 1/2 in.   303
Unarranged.

U. Operations Service, 1943-45

This service was concerned primarily with supervising the
construction and operation of military hospitals in the United States
during World War II, the evacuation of wounded personnel from overseas,
and the distribution of patients.

1. General Records

SECURITY-CLASSIFIED DIARIES. Oct. 1943-Dec. 1945. 3 ft.   304
Arranged chronologically.

2. Medical Regulating Unit

The Medical Regulating Unit advised the Office of the
Chief of Transportation on problems relating to the evacuation by ship
of wounded and sick personnel from oversea points during World War II.

HOSPITAL SHIP PLATOON DATA CARDS. 1943-45. 9 in.   305
Arranged numerically by platoon number.

V. Office Service Division, 1944-46

The Office Service Division procured office supplies, equipment, and reproduction services, issued administrative orders, maintained the central files, and was responsible for records administration
in the Surgeon General's Office and its field agencies during World
War II.

RECORDS RELATING TO THE "SGO ORGANIZATIONAL MANUAL PROJECT." 1944.
2 ft.   306
Unarranged.

RECORDS RELATING TO THE 1946 REORGANIZATION OF THE SURGEON GENERAL'S
OFFICE. 1946. 5 in.   307
Unarranged.

III. Army Medical Examining Boards Convened in Various Cities

For records relating to earlier Army medical examining boards
(1832-61), see series 13.

A. Washington, D.C., 1862-1901

PROCEEDINGS OF THE ARMY MEDICAL EXAMINING BOARD ESTABLISHED TO EXAMINE
CANDIDATES FOR APPOINTMENT AS BRIGADE SURGEONS. June 1862-Apr. 1865.
1 vol. 1 in.   <u>308</u>
Arranged chronologically.

MERIT ROLLS OF SURGEONS AND ASSISTANT SURGEONS EXAMINED BY THE ARMY
MEDICAL EXAMINING BOARD. 1862-65. 1 vol. 1 in.   <u>309</u>
Arranged chronologically. Name index.

PROCEEDINGS OF THE ARMY MEDICAL BOARD ESTABLISHED TO EXAMINE APPLICANTS
FOR APPOINTMENT AS MEDICAL OFFICERS IN THE FIRST ARMY CORPS.
Dec. 1864-June 1865. 1 vol. 1 in.   <u>310</u>
Arranged chronologically.

LETTERS SENT BY THE ARMY MEDICAL EXAMINING BOARD OF DENTAL SURGEONS.
Feb.-July 1901. 1 in.   <u>311</u>
Arranged chronologically. Name index.

REGISTER OF LETTERS RECEIVED BY THE ARMY MEDICAL EXAMINING BOARD OF
DENTAL SURGEONS. Feb.-July 1901. 1 vol. 1 in.   <u>312</u>
Arranged chronologically by date of receipt.

B. <u>Cincinnati, Ohio: Army Medical Examining Board Established
to Examine Candidates for Appointment as Assistant
Surgeons of Volunteers, 1863-65.</u>

MINUTES OF MEETINGS June 1863-May 1865. 3 vols. 3 in.   <u>313</u>
Arranged chronologically.

LETTERS SENT. June 1863-Apr. 1865. 1 vol. 1 in.   <u>314</u>
Arranged chronologically.

LIST OF CANDIDATES EXAMINED. June 1863-Apr. 1865. 1 vol. 1 in.   <u>315</u>
Arranged chronologically by date of examination.

C. <u>New York, N.Y.: Army Medical Examining Boards Established
to Examine Candidates Seeking Appointment as Assistant
Surgeons and to Examine Assistant Surgeons for Promotion
to the Rank of Surgeon, 1865-96</u>

Each of several successive boards was established whenever there
were enough applicants to warrant a new board, and each board dissolved
itself after the examinations were completed. Each board therefore was
a separate entity, possibly differing in composition from the others,
and maintained its own records.

REGISTER OF CANDIDATES INVITED TO APPEAR BEFORE ARMY MEDICAL EXAMINING
   BOARDS IN NEW YORK CITY. Sept. 1865-Sept. 1896. 1 vol. 2 in.   316
   Arranged chronologically by date of boards. Index to names of
candidates.

LETTERS AND ENDORSEMENTS SENT. Sept. 1866-Oct. 1867. 1 vol.
   1/2 in.
   Arranged chronologically.   317

REPORTS OF EXAMINATIONS OF REJECTED CANDIDATES. Sept. 1866-Oct. 1867.
   2 vols. 1 in.
   Arranged chronologically by date of candidate's examination.   318

PROCEEDINGS. Mar.-Dec. 1868. 1 vol. 1 in.   319
   Arranged chronologically.

REPORTS OF EXAMINATIONS. May-Nov. 1868. 1 vol. 1/2 in.   320
   Arranged chronologically. Index to names of examinees.

JOURNAL OF PROCEEDINGS. July 1874-Dec. 1876. 2 vols. 2 in.   321
   Arranged chronologically.

LETTERS SENT. Aug. 1874-Dec. 1876. 1 vol. 1/2 in.   322
   Arranged chronologically.

REPORTS OF EXAMINATIONS. 1874-76. 2 vols. 1 in.   323
   Arranged chronologically.

JOURNAL OF PROCEEDINGS. Oct. 1877-June 1882. 3 vols. 3 in.   324
   Arranged chronologically.

LETTERS SENT. Oct. 1877-June 1882. 2 vols. 2 in.   325
   Arranged chronologically. Volume 2 has a name index.

REPORTS OF EXAMINATIONS. Mar. 1877-May 1882. 3 vols. 3 in.   326
   Arranged chronologically. Volume 3 has a name index to candidates.

MINUTES OF MEETINGS. Feb. 1883-June 1884. 1 vol. 1 in.   327
   Arranged chronologically.

LETTERS SENT. Feb. 1883-June 1884. 1 vol. 1 in.   328
   Arranged chronologically. Name index.

REGISTER OF LETTERS RECEIVED. Sept. 1883-May 1884. 1 vol. 1/4 in. 329
   Arranged chronologically by date of receipt. The entries are
numbered consecutively.

REPORTS OF EXAMINATIONS. Mar. 1883-June 1884. 1 vol. 1 in.   330
   Arranged chronologically.

MINUTES OF MEETINGS. Apr. 1885-Apr. 1887. 1 vol. 1 in.   331
   Arranged chronologically.

LETTERS SENT. Apr. 1885-Apr. 1887. 2 vols. 2 in.   332
   Arranged chronologically. Name index in each volume.

LETTERS RECEIVED. Feb. 1886-Mar. 1887. 1 vol. 1 in.   333
   Arranged chronologically. Name index to correspondents.

ENDORSEMENTS SENT. Feb. 1886-Mar. 1887. 1 vol. 1 in.   334
   Arranged chronologically.

REPORT OF EXAMINATIONS. Apr. 1885-Mar. 1887. 1 vol. 1 in.   335
   Arranged chronologically. Name index to candidates.

LETTERS RECEIVED RELATING TO THE EXAMINATION OF A NEW TYPE OF
   AMBULANCE. Mar.-July 1891. 2 in.   336
   Arranged chronologically by date of receipt and numbered
consecutively.

   D.   San Francisco, Calif.: Army Medical Examining Board
        Established to Examine Candidates Seeking Appointment
        as Assistant Surgeons and to Examine Assistant Surgeons
        for Promotion to the Rank of Surgeon, 1874-75

PROCEEDINGS. July 1874-Apr. 1875. 1 vol. 1 in.   337
   Arranged chronologically. Name index.

NAME AND SUBJECT INDEX TO SERIES 339. 1 vol. 1/4 in.   338

LETTERS SENT. Aug. 1874-Apr. 1875. 1 vol. 1/2 in.   339
   Arranged chronologically. For a name and subject index see
series 338.

NAME INDEX TO SERIES 341. 1 vol. 1/2 in.   340

LETTERS RECEIVED. July 1874-Apr. 1875. 1 vol. 1/2 in.   341
   Arranged chronologically. For a name index see series 340.

E. <u>Chicago, Ill.: Army Medical Examining Board Established to Examine Candidates Seeking Appointment as Assistant Surgeons and to Examine Assistant Surgeons for Promotion to the Rank of Surgeon, 1891-92.</u>

LETTER BOOK. Jan.-Feb. 1892. 1 vol. 1 in. <u>342</u>
   Arranged in two subseries: letters sent and letters received. The former is arranged chronologically by date of dispatch, and the latter by date of receipt.

LETTERS RECEIVED. 1891-92. 1 in. <u>343</u>
   Arranged and numbered in chronological order.

IV. <u>Medical Department Field Installations</u>

   A. <u>General Hospitals</u>

      1. <u>Army and Navy General Hospital, Hot Springs, Ark., 1886-1939</u>

         The Army and Navy General Hospital was established by an act of Congress of June 30, 1882 (22 Stat. 121). The hospital received its first patients in January 1887.

ANNUAL REPORTS. 1930-31; 1933-39. 2 in. <u>344</u>
   Arranged chronologically.

SPECIAL ORDERS. 1939. 2 in. <u>345</u>
   Arranged chronologically.

MONTHLY RETURNS. 1898-1912. 1 ft. <u>346</u>
   Arranged chronologically.

MUSTER ROLLS. 1887-1918. 2 ft. <u>347</u>
   Arranged chronologically.

REGISTER OF CIVILIAN EMPLOYEES. 1886-88. 1 vol. 1 in. <u>348</u>
   Arranged chronologically by date of appointment.

MEDICAL CASE FILES OF PATIENTS ("CLINICAL RECORDS"). Mar. 1890- <u>349</u>
   Oct. 1912. 61 ft.
   Arranged alphabetically by name of patient.

REGISTER OF APPLICATIONS FOR ADMISSION. Jan. 1887-Nov. 1889. <u>350</u>
   1 vol. 1 in.
   Arranged chronologically.

REGISTER OF PATIENTS AND CONSOLIDATED REPORT OF THE MEDICAL
   DEPARTMENT. 1887-1906. 5 vols. 8 in. <u>351</u>
   Arranged chronologically.

MONTHLY STATEMENTS OF ACCOUNT CURRENT OF THE DISBURSING OFFICER.
    1888-1906. 1 vol. 2 in.   352
    Arranged chronologically. Name index.

SUBSISTENCE ACCOUNTS. 1887-88. 1 vol. 1/2 in.   353
    Arranged chronologically.

2. Letterman General Hospital, San Francisco, Calif., 1898-1913

        This hospital, located on the Presidio of San Francisco
military reservation, was established as Army General Hospital, San
Francisco, on December 1, 1898, to care for the sick and wounded
returning from the Philippine Islands. In 1911 it was named in honor
of Jonathan Letterman, who had been the Medical Director of the Army
of the Potomac.

LETTERS AND ENDORSEMENTS SENT. June 1898-Sept. 1906. 36 vols.
    6 ft.   354
    Arranged and numbered in chronological order, except for those
in the first four volumes, which are not numbered. The first volume
contains letters received for June-July 1898.

NAME INDEX TO PART (AUG. 1906-JAN. 1907) OF SERIES 356. 1 vol.
    1/2 in.   355

LETTERS AND ENDORSEMENTS SENT, HOSPITAL CORPS DETACHMENT. 1901-7.
    2 vols. 2 in.   356
    Arranged and numbered in chronological order. For a partial name
index see series 355.

LETTERS SENT, OFFICE OF THE DENTAL SURGEON. Apr. 1905-Dec. 1912.
    1 vol. 1 in.   357
    Arranged chronologically.

LETTERS RECEIVED. Aug. 1898. 1 vol. 1 in.   358
    Arranged chronologically. Name index. Letters received for
June-July 1898 are in volume 1 of series 354.

REGISTERS OF LETTERS AND ENDORSEMENTS RECEIVED. Aug. 1898-Sept. 1906.
    22 vols. 3 ft.   359
    Arranged chronologically by period and thereunder generally by
date of receipt. The entries are numbered consecutively. Name
index in each volume.

REGISTERS OF CORRESPONDENCE. Sept. 1906-Apr. 1908; Sept. 1908-Oct. Oct. 1909. 9 vols. 1 ft. 360
   Arranged chronologically by periods, and thereunder by date of receipt. The entries are numbered consecutively.

LETTERS AND ENDORSEMENTS RECEIVED, HOSPITAL CORPS DETACHMENT. 361
   Mar. 1901-Jan. 1907. 1 vol. 2 in.
   Arranged chronologically by date of receipt. Name index.

LETTERS SENT BY MAJ. W.SS. MATTHEWS, BRIGADE SURGEON COMMANDING THE 362
   HOSPITAL. Apr.-July 1899. 2 vols. 2 in.
   Arranged chronologically. Name index in each volume.

CORRESPONDENCE AND RELATED RECORDS PERTAINING TO THE SAN FRANCISCO 363
   EARTHQUAKE AND FIRE. 1906. 5 in.
   Unarranged.

GENERAL ORDERS. 1900-1903. 2 vols. 2 in. 364
   Arranged chronologically by year and thereunder numerically.
Name and subject index in each volume.

SPECIAL ORDERS. Dec. 1898-Jan. 1904. 7 vols. 1 ft. 365
   Arranged by year and thereunder numerically. Name index in each
volume.

CIRCULARS. Jan. 1900-Jan. 1904. 2 vols. 2 in. 366
   Arranged chronologically by year and thereunder numerically.

MEMORANDUM CIRCULARS. Apr. 1901-Oct. 1903. 1 vol. 1 in. 367
   Arranged chronologically.

REGISTER OF PHYSICAL EXAMINATIONS OF RECRUITS. Oct. 1898-July 1908. 368
   1 vol. 1 in.
   Arranged chronologically by month.

NAME INDEXES TO REGULAR ARMY PATIENTS (1898-1906; 1909-10) IN 369
   SERIES 372. 9 vols. 1 ft.

NAME INDEX TO VOLUNTEER ARMY PATIENTS (CA. 1898-1901) IN SERIES 370
   372. 1 vol. 1 in.

NAME INDEX TO CIVILIANS IN SERIES 372 HOSPITALIZED AS A RESULT OF
   THE SAN FRANCISCO EARTHQUAKE AND FIRE OF APRIL 18, 1906. 1 vol.
   1 in. 371

REGISTERS OF PATIENTS. June 1898-Feb. 1907. 5 vols. 6 in. 372
   Arranged chronologically by date of admission to hospital and
numbered consecutively.

MEDICAL CASE FILES OF PATIENTS ("CLINICAL RECORDS"). 1898-1913. 385 ft. 373

Arranged numerically by case number. Partially indexed in series 369 and 370; partially registered in series 372.

MUSTER ROLLS OF PATIENTS. 1898-1908. 4 ft. 374

Arranged chronologically.

REGISTERS OF DEATHS AND INTERMENTS OF PATIENTS. June 1898-Apr. 1910. 19 vols. 8 in. 375

Arranged chronologically. Name index in each volume.

UNIDENTIFIED NAME INDEXES TO CORRESPONDENCE. 2 vols. 1/2 in. 376

3. Army General Hospital, Fort Bayard, N. Mex., 1899-1912

Fort Bayard was established on August 21, 1866, to protect the miners in that area of the Territory of New Mexico from the Warm Spring Apaches under Victorio. In January 1900 Fort Bayard was discontinued as a garrisoned post and turned over to the Surgeon General of the Army for use as a sanatorium for the treatment of officers and enlisted men suffering from pulmonary tuberculosis. In 1920 the hospital was transferred to the Public Health Service.

LETTERS AND ENDORSEMENTS SENT. Dec. 1899-Jan. 1903. 4 vols. 8 in. 377

Arranged chronologically. Name index in each volume.

PRESS COPIES OF LETTERS SENT. Oct. 1899-Apr. 1903. 9 vols. 1 ft. 378

Arranged chronologically.

NAME AND SUBJECT INDEXES TO SERIES 380. 2 vols. 1/4 in. 379

LETTERS SENT. 1905-6. 9 vols. 1 ft. 380

Arranged chronologically. For name and subject indexes see series 379.

REGISTER OF LETTERS RECEIVED. May-Aug. 1906. 1 vol. 2 in. 381

Arranged chronologically by date of receipt. The entries are numbered consecutively.

LETTERS RECEIVED. 1900-1906. 4 ft. 382

Arranged by year and thereunder arranged and numbered in chronological order by date of receipt. For a partial register see series 381.

NAME AND SUBJECT INDEX TO SERIES 386. 3 ft. 383

Card index.

NAME AND SUBJECT INDEXES TO SERIES 386. 3 vols. 6 in. <u>384</u>

REGISTERS OF CORRESPONDENCE. 1906; 1908-11. 4 vols. 6 in. <u>385</u>
     Arranged chronologically by date of receipt. The entries are
numbered consecutively.

GENERAL CORRESPONDENCE. 1906-12. 43 ft. <u>386</u>
     Arranged and numbered in chronological order in two subseries:
1906-11 and 1912. Indexed in series 383 and 384; partly registered
in series 385.

CORRESPONDENCE RELATING TO WATER AND WATER RIGHTS ("WATER LANDS").
     1906-10. 2 in. <u>387</u>
     Arranged chronologically. Name index.

REGISTER OF CORRESPONDENCE OF THE CONSTRUCTING QUARTERMASTER.
     1911-12. 1 vol. 1 in. <u>388</u>
     Arranged chronologically. The entries are numbered consecutively.

GENERAL ORDERS. 1902-12. 3 in. <u>389</u>
     Arranged by year and thereunder numerically.

SPECIAL ORDERS. 1903-12. 6 in. <u>390</u>
     Arranged by year and thereunder numerically.

CIRCULARS. 1904-12. 2 in. <u>391</u>
     Arranged by year and thereunder numerically.

MONTHLY RETURNS. 1904-12. 6 in. <u>392</u>
     Arranged chronologically.

MONTHLY RETURNS OF THE HOSPITAL CORPS DETACHMENT. 1903-10. 1 ft. <u>393</u>
     Arranged chronologically.

MONTHLY RETURNS OF U.S. SOLDIERS' HOME PATIENTS. 1912. 3 in. <u>394</u>
     Arranged chronologically.

REGISTERS OF PATIENTS. 1899-1907. 2 vols. 1 in. <u>395</u>
     Arranged numerically by case number. Name index in each volume.

MEDICAL CASE FILES ("CLINICAL RECORDS"). 1900-1912. 33 ft. <u>396</u>
     Arranged alphabetically by name of patient.

CASE HISTORIES OF PATIENTS. 1901-4; 10 vols. 1 ft. <u>397</u>
     Arranged numerically by case number (441-1128, with some gaps).

UNDATED NAME INDEXES TO U.S. SOLDIERS' HOME PATIENTS. 3 vols.
   1/4 in.   <u>398</u>
   Registers not found.

MISCELLANEOUS RECORDS. 1900-1912. 10 in.   <u>399</u>
   Unarranged.

UNIDENTIFIED NAME AND SUBJECT INDEX. 1 vol. 1/4 in.   <u>400</u>

4. <u>Walter Reed General Hospital, Washington, D.C. 1909-19</u>

        As early as 1862 Surgeon General Hammond pointed out the need for a permanent general hospital in the Washington area. Nothing was done, however, until September 1898, when the post hospital at Washington Barracks was designated as a general hospital. Facilities in this temporary building proved inadequate, and by 1903 the Medical Department was seeking a site upon which to construct a modern hospital.

        In May 1905 the War Department purchased land in Takoma Park for this purpose. Construction soon began, and on May 1, 1909, Walter Reed General Hospital, named after Maj. Walter Reed, whose research work led to the control of yellow fever, was opened. In 1923 the hospital became a part of the Army Medical Center.

ANNUAL REPORTS. 1911-19. 3 in.   <u>401</u>
   Arranged chronologically.

MUSTER ROLLS. 1911. 2 in.   <u>402</u>
   Arranged chronologically.

RETURNS OF THE HOSPITAL CORPS DETACHMENT. Nov. 1911-Sept. 1912.
   1/4 in.   <u>403</u>
   Arranged chronologically.

MEDICAL CASE FILES OF PATIENTS ("CLINICAL RECORDS"). 1909-12.
   40 ft.   <u>404</u>
   Arranged by case number.

B. <u>Medical Supply Depots, 1864-1917</u>

LETTERS SENT BY MAJ. CHARLES B. WHITE, ASSISTANT MEDICAL PURVEYOR,
   NEW ORLEANS MEDICAL SUPPLY DEPOT, LA. 1865-68. 2 vols. 2 in.   <u>405</u>
   Arranged chronologically. Name index in each volume.

LETTERS SENT BY CAPT. FLORENCE O'DONNOGHUE, MEDICAL STOREKEEPER,
   NEW ORLEANS MEDICAL SUPPLY DEPOT, LA. 1868-70. 1 vol. 1 in.   <u>406</u>
   Arranged chronologically. Name index.

LETTERS RECEIVED BY MAJ. CHARLES B. WHITE, ASSISTANT MEDICAL PURVEYOR, NEW ORLEANS MEDICAL SUPPLY DEPOT, LA. 1864-66. 1 vol. 2 in. 407
Unarranged.

ACCOUNT OF RECEIPTS AND ISSUES OF MEDICAL AND HOSPITAL SUPPLIES, NEW ORLEANS MEDICAL SUPPLY DEPOT, LA. 1864-65. 18 vols. 6 in. 408
Arranged chronologically.

LETTERS SENT BY THE ATLANTA MEDICAL SUPPLY DEPOT, GA. 1898-99. 2 vols. 2 in. 409
Arranged chronologically. Name index.

LETTERS SENT BY THE SAVANNAH MEDICAL SUPPLY DEPOT, GA. 1898-1900. 2 vols. 3 in. 410
Arranged chronologically. Name index in each volume.

REGISTER OF LETTERS RECEIVED BY THE SAVANNAH MEDICAL SUPPLY DEPOT, GA. Apr.-1899-Jan. 1900. 1 vol. 2 in. 411
Arranged chronologically. The entries are numbered consecutively.

LETTERS, TELEGRAMS, AND ENDORSEMENTS SENT BY THE HUNTSVILLE MEDICAL SUPPLY DEPOT, ALA. Sept. 1898-Mar. 1899. 1 vol. 1 in. 412
Arranged chronologically.

LETTERS AND ENDORSEMENTS RECEIVED BY THE MANILA MEDICAL SUPPLY DEPOT, DEPARTMENT OF NORTHERN LUZON, P.I. 1900-1901. 1 vol. 1 in. 413
Arranged chronologically by date of receipt. Name index to correspondents.

TELEGRAMS RECEIVED BY THE MANILA MEDICAL SUPPLY DEPOT, DEPARTMENT OF SOUTHERN LUZON, P.I. June 1900-Sept. 1901. 1 vol. 2 in. 414
Arranged chronologically. Name index.

CORRESPONDENCE OF THE MEDICAL DEPOT AT ARSENAL, HAVANA, CUBA. 1906-8. 9 in. 415
Unarranged.

CORRESPONDENCE OF THE EL PASO MEDICAL SUPPLY DEPOT, TEX. 1916-17. 8 in. 416
Arranged according to the War Department decimal classification scheme.

C. Miscellaneous Installations, 1859-1939

INVOICES OF SUPPLIES ISSUED BY THE MEDICAL PURVEYOR AT BENECIA BARRACKS, CALIF. 1859-61. 1 vol. 1/2 in. 417
Arranged chronologically.

INVOICES OF MEDICAL PROPERTY ISSUED BY THE MEDICAL PURVEYOR'S OFFICE, HARRISON'S POINT, VA. July-Sept. 1862. 2 vols. 2 in. 418
Arranged chronologically.

LETTERS SENT BY THE MEDICAL SUBPURVEYING DEPOT, FORT YUMA, CALIF. Feb. 1873-Nov. 1876. 1 vol. 1 in. 419
Arranged chronologically. Name index.

CORRESPONDENCE, REPORTS, AND STUDIES RELATING TO TYPHOID VACCINES, VACCINE DEPARTMENT, ARMY MEDICAL SCHOOL. 1912-39. 2 ft. 420
Unarranged.

SUMMARY DATA CARDS RELATING TO THE PRODUCTION AND TESTING OF TYPHOID VACCINES, VACCINE DEPARTMENT, ARMY MEDICAL SCHOOL. 1912-39. 8 in. 421
Arranged by subject.

CORRESPONDENCE RELATING TO CIVILIAN PERSONNEL, MEDICAL SUPPLY OFFICE, NORFOLK QUARTERMASTER INTERMEDIATE DEPOT, VA. 1920-22. 3 in. 422
Unarranged.

V. Military Organizations

  A. Military Departments, 1862-69

REGISTER OF SERVICE OF CONTRACT SURGEONS, DEPARTMENT OF THE GULF. 1862-65. 1 vol. 1 in. 423
Arranged chronologically. Name index.

LETTERS AND ENDORSEMENTS SENT REGARDING ARTIFICIAL LIMBS, DEPARTMENT OF THE EAST. Mar. 1864-Mar. 1869. 2 vols. 2 in. 424
Arranged chronologically.

  B. Field Units, 1862-99

LETTERS SENT BY ASSISTANT SURGEON R. H. ALEXANDER, MEDICAL PURVEYOR, ARMY OF THE POTOMAC. 1862. 1 vol. 1 in. 425
Arranged chronologically.

REPORT OF LT. COL. A. C. GIRARD, CHIEF SURGEON, 2D ARMY CORPS. 1898. 1 vol. 1 in. 426

REGISTER OF LETTERS AND ENDORSEMENTS RECEIVED, 2D DIVISION HOSPITAL, 2D ARMY CORPS. 1898-99. 1 vol. 1 in. 427
Arranged chronologically by date of receipt. The entries are numbered consecutively.

REGISTER OF SERVICE OF CONTRACT NURSES WITH THE 2D DIVISION HOSPITAL, 2D ARMY CORPS. 1898-99. 1 vol. 1/2 in. 428
Arranged chronologically. Name index.

APPENDIX I

SUBJECT - ALPHABETIC CLASSIFICATION SCHEME, 1917-37
(USED IN SERIES 31)

A	Ambulance Companies
B	Flying Fields and Schools
C	Camps
D	Cantonments
E	States, Cities, and Countries
G	Divisions
H	Hospital Trains
I	Hospitals (auxiliary camp, convalescent, debarkation, embarkation, and veterinary)
J	Base Hospitals
K	General Hospitals
L	Field Hospitals
M	Medical Supply Depots
N	Posts
P	Sanitary Inspection Reports
Q	Sanitary Trains
R	Remount Depots
T	Societies and Associations
V	Miscellaneous Units
W	Colleges
X	Periodicals
Y	American Expeditionary Forces
Z	Mobile Hospitals
AA	Military Departments
BB	Ships
CC	Army Corps
DD	Hospital Funds
EE	Laboratories
GG	Institutions

APPENDIX II

SUBJECT-ALPHABETIC CLASSIFICATION SCHEME, 1938-46
(USED IN SERIES 31 AND 32)

B	Army Air Force and Fields
C	Camps
E	Armies and Corps
F	Countries and States
G	Divisions
H	Hospital Trains
I	Station Hospitals
J	Base Hospitals
K	General Hospitals
L	Field Hospitals
M	Depots
N	Posts, Forts, and Arsenals
R	Remount Depots
T	Societies and Associations
V	Medical Schools, Miscellaneous Units
W	Schools and Colleges
X	Newspapers and Magazines
Y	A. P. O.
AA	Military Departments
BB	Ships
CC	Staff Corps and Arms of Services
EE	Laboratories
GG	S. G. O., Army Medical Center, Army Library, and Army School
OO	Geographic Codes (used mainly by Classified Section)

www.ingramcontent.com/pod-product-compliance
Lightning Source LLC
Chambersburg PA
CBHW081547040426
42448CB00015B/3244